Teaching Children to PRAY

Ages 4 & 5

Rainbow Publishers®

P.O. Box 70130 • Richmond, VA 23255
www.rainbowpublishers.com

Teaching Children to PRAY

Ages 4 & 5

Mary J. Davis

Dedication

To my precious sisters in Christ: Carol, Yvonne, and Candy.

TEACHING CHILDREN TO PRAY: AGES 4&5

ISBN 10: 1-885358-24-5
ISBN 13: 978-1-885358-24-0
Rainbow reorder #RB36612
RELIGION / Christian Ministry / Children

Rainbow Publishers
P.O. Box 261129
San Diego, CA 92196
www.rainbowpublishers.com

Interior Illustrator: Michael Talbot
Cover Illustrator: Terry Julien

Printed in the United States of America

CONTENTS

Memory Verse Index 6
Materials to Gather 7
Preface 9

Prayers for Care

Care Card 11
Feathered Friend Feeder 13
God's Umbrella 15
Happy Flyers 17
Jesus and Children Ribbon Mobile 19
Jonah Shape Book 21
Noah Sponge Painting 23
Fuzzy Sheep Plaque 25
Trust 'N' Tie Bookmark 27

Prayers of Commitment

Ears to Listen to God 29
Find the Good Food 31
Follow Jesus Windsock 33
Gentle Bubbles 35
Helper Magnets 37
Missions Shoe Bank 39
Prayer Poster 41
Rocking Sheep 43
Walking in Love 45
Worship God Napkin Rings 47
Worship Picture Puzzle 49

Prayers of Praise

Creation Straw Sippers 51
Easter Garland 53
Happy Frog 55
Magnifying Glass Game 57
My Butterfly 59
Nature Book 61
Persistent Prayer Puzzle 63
Praise Pendant 65
Praise the Lord Wind Chimes 67
Prayer Buddy 69
Stained Glass Window 71
Star Praise 73

Prayers of Thanks

Call on God 75
Five Times to Pray 77
Harvest Wreath 79
Image Mirror 81
Jesus Feeds 5,000 83
Never Alone Switch Covers 85
Prayer Place Cards 87
Summer Fun Visor 89
Thank-You Chain 91
Thankful Kite 93
Thanksgiving Prayer Book 95

MEMORY VERSE INDEX

Genesis 1:14 .... *Summer Fun Visor* 89
Genesis 1:27 .... *Image Mirror* 81
Genesis 1:29 .... *Harvest Wreath* 79
Genesis 8:1 .... *Noah Sponge Painting* 23
1 Samuel 2:1 .... *Persistent Prayer Puzzle* 63
1 Chronicles 16:9 .... *Prayer Buddy* 69
Psalm 23:1 .... *Fuzzy Sheep Plaque* 25
Psalm 66:5 .... *Nature Book* 61
Psalm 100:3 .... *Rocking Sheep* 43
Psalm 135:3 .... *My Butterfly* 59
Psalm 136:1 .... *Thankful Kite* 93
Psalm 148:3 .... *Star Praise* 73
Proverbs 20:11 .... *Helper Magnets* 37
Isaiah 12:2 .... *Trust 'N' Tie Bookmark* 27
Jonah 2:2 .... *Jonah Shape Book* 21
Nahum 1:7 .... *God's Umbrella* 15
Matthew 4:19 .... *Follow Jesus Windsock* 33
Matthew 5:12 .... *Happy Frog* 55
Matthew 7:7 .... *Five Times to Pray* 77
Matthew 14:19 .... *Jesus Feeds 5,000* 83
Matthew 19:14 .... *Jesus and Children Ribbon Mobile* 19
Matthew 21:9 .... *Praise the Lord Wind Chimes* 67
Matthew 21:22 .... *Prayer Place Cards* 87
Matthew 28:19 .... *Missions Shoe Bank* 39
Matthew 28:20 .... *Never Alone Switch Covers* 85
Mark 16:6 .... *Easter Garland* 53
Luke 1:46 .... *Magnifying Glass Game* 57
Luke 4:8 .... *Worship Picture Puzzle* 49
Luke 6:12 .... *Stained Glass Window* 71
Luke 11:28 .... *Ears to Listen to God* 29
Luke 12:7 .... *Feathered Friend Feeder* 13
Acts 17:24 .... *Creation Straw Sippers* 51
1 Corinthians 3:16 .... *Find the Good Food* 31
Ephesians 4:2 .... *Gentle Bubbles* 35
Philippians 4:19 .... *Happy Flyers* 17
Colossians 4:2 .... *Prayer Poster* 41
1 Thessalonians 5:18 .... *Thanksgiving Prayer Book* 95
2 Timothy 1:3 .... *Thank-You Chain* 91
James 5:16 .... *Care Card* 11
1 John 4:19 .... *Praise Pendant* 65
1 John 5:14 .... *Call on God* 75
2 John 1:6 .... *Walking in Love* 45
Revelation 22:9 .... *Worship God Napkin Rings* 47

MATERIALS TO GATHER

Because these activities are especially designed for 4s & 5s, they require little work beyond simple cutting, coloring and gluing. Listed below are all of the items you will need to lead the activities as they are designed in this book. However, you may eliminate and add as you desire. Use the reproducible note at the bottom of the page to obtain volunteer help in collecting materials. Check off each item as you receive it. You may wish to use a pair of adult scissors to pre-cut any crafts and avoid confusion with preschoolers who may not yet be proficient with scissors. If you do allow them to cut, be sure to use children's safety scissors. All activities calling for "tape" require the clear type of tape.

- ❑ aluminum foil
- ❑ boxes, small pudding or gelatin
- ❑ card stock or heavy paper
- ❑ chenille stems
- ❑ clothespins, spring-type
- ❑ construction paper
- ❑ cotton balls
- ❑ craft sticks
- ❑ crayons
- ❑ dish soap, liquid
- ❑ envelopes
- ❑ foam or paper cups
- ❑ foam plates or meat trays
- ❑ glue
- ❑ leaves
- ❑ hole punch
- ❑ hole reinforcements
- ❑ juice cans
- ❑ juice can lids, metal
- ❑ magnet strips
- ❑ markers, permanent
- ❑ marshmallows, white miniature
- ❑ napkins, paper
- ❑ paint, blue tempera or acrylic
- ❑ paper plates
- ❑ pencils
- ❑ plastic drinking straws
- ❑ poster board
- ❑ ribbon or paper streamers
- ❑ sandwich bags, plastic zipper-type
- ❑ scissors, adult
- ❑ scissors, safety
- ❑ seed, bird
- ❑ sponge, small pieces
- ❑ stickers, foil star
- ❑ tape
- ❑ transparencies, clear
- ❑ tissue paper, bright-colored
- ❑ yarn

To Families and Friends of 4s & 5s

We are planning many special craft activities for your child. Some of these crafts include regular household items. We would like to ask your help in saving the items checked below for our activities.

- ❑ aluminum foil
- ❑ boxes, small pudding or gelatin
- ❑ chenille stems
- ❑ clothespins, spring-type
- ❑ cotton balls
- ❑ envelopes
- ❑ foam or paper cups
- ❑ foam plates or meat trays
- ❑ juice cans
- ❑ juice can lids, metal
- ❑ marshmallows, white miniature
- ❑ napkins, paper
- ❑ paper plates
- ❑ plastic drinking straws
- ❑ popsicle sticks
- ❑ ribbon or paper streamers
- ❑ sandwich bags, plastic zipper-type
- ❑ seed, bird
- ❑ sponge, small pieces
- ❑ tissue paper, bright-colored
- ❑ yarn

Please bring the items on ______________________________. Thank you for your help!

PREFACE

Prayer is our lifeline to God. Without prayer, we falter in our walk with Him and give in to worries, fears and even temptations. The time to begin building a powerful prayer life is in early childhood, for children who learn the power of prayer early will have a special relationship with their Lord.

The activities in this book will help students build that strong prayer life. These projects offer a variety of activities to keep students interested while adding to the building blocks of their faith and prayer lives. The projects have been designed with flexibility to serve as independent lessons or as add-ons to your curriculum. They can also be used in Christian schools or at home as family devotional projects. To make selection of the appropriate activity easier, the projects are grouped in four sections: Prayers for Care, Prayers of Commitment, Prayers of Praise and Prayers of Thanks – allowing the teacher or parent to emphasize topics of prayer. Also, on page six you will find a memory verse index, allowing you to choose an activity that applies to a particular verse your class may be studying.

Within each activity description, you are provided with everything you need to teach a prayer lesson: memory verse, prayer thought (or theme), suggested prayer, materials list, pre-class preparation and step-by-step instructions. Each project includes reproducible patterns or illustrations, as well as a related lesson idea with a scripture reference. All activities have been especially designed to meet the abilities and interests of 4s & 5s while also offering a teacher-friendly concept that makes lessons a breeze to prepare and teach – making class time less hectic and more rewarding for both you and the children.

Since all of these activities are about prayer, it is important both for the adult to lead in prayer and for the children to be encouraged to pray in class. Soon, your children will look forward to prayer time as they work on these exciting activities. What a wonderful foundation to begin and build upon with your students!

CARE CARD

Prayer Thought

I will pray for others.

Memory Verse

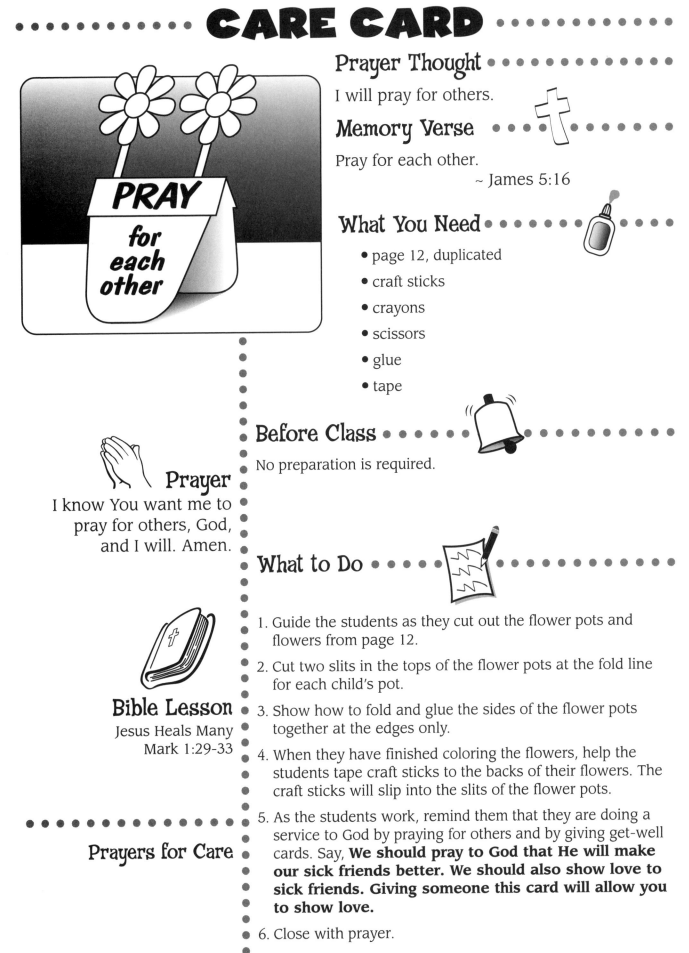

Pray for each other.

~ James 5:16

What You Need

- page 12, duplicated
- craft sticks
- crayons
- scissors
- glue
- tape

Before Class

No preparation is required.

What to Do

1. Guide the students as they cut out the flower pots and flowers from page 12.
2. Cut two slits in the tops of the flower pots at the fold line for each child's pot.
3. Show how to fold and glue the sides of the flower pots together at the edges only.
4. When they have finished coloring the flowers, help the students tape craft sticks to the backs of their flowers. The craft sticks will slip into the slits of the flower pots.
5. As the students work, remind them that they are doing a service to God by praying for others and by giving get-well cards. Say, **We should pray to God that He will make our sick friends better. We should also show love to sick friends. Giving someone this card will allow you to show love.**
6. Close with prayer.

Prayer

I know You want me to pray for others, God, and I will. Amen.

Bible Lesson

Jesus Heals Many
Mark 1:29-33

Prayers for Care

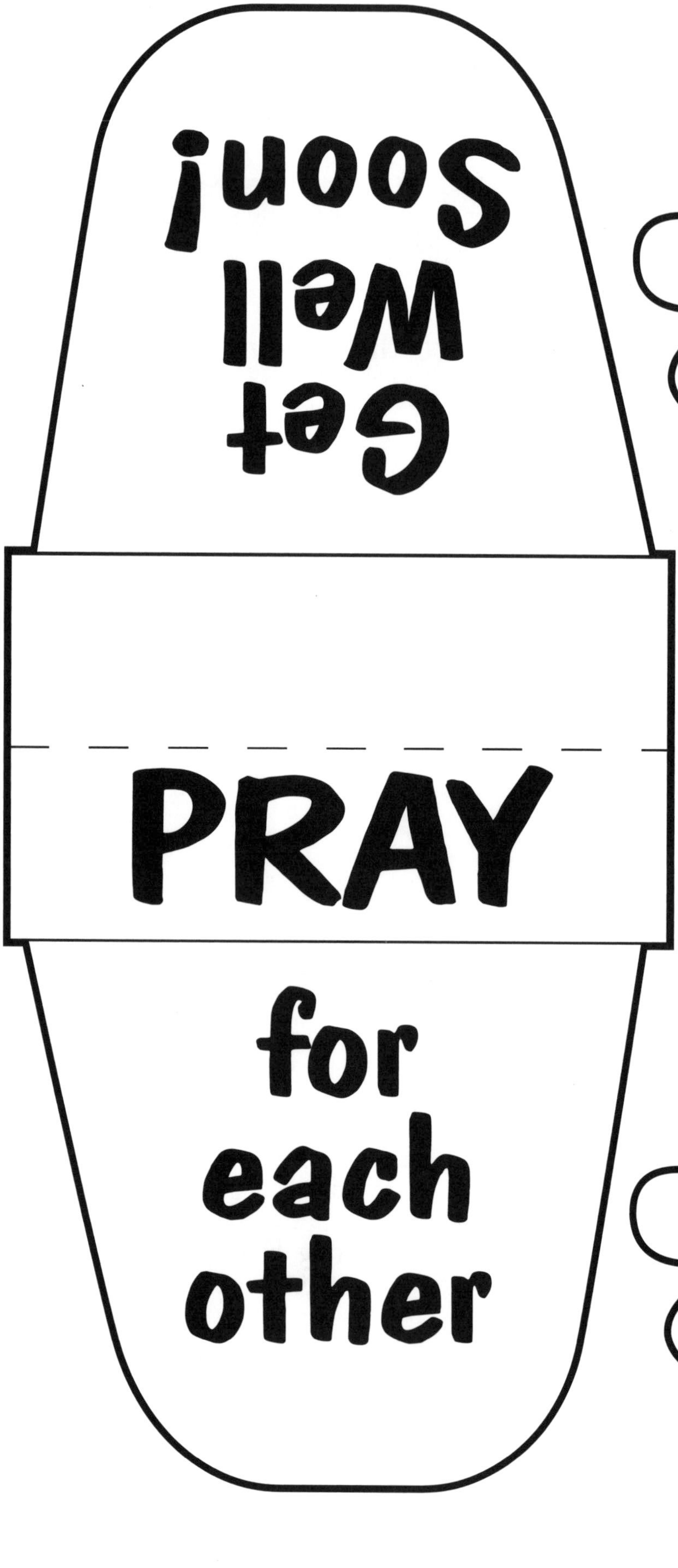
Get Well Soon!
PRAY
for each other

FEATHERED FRIEND FEEDER

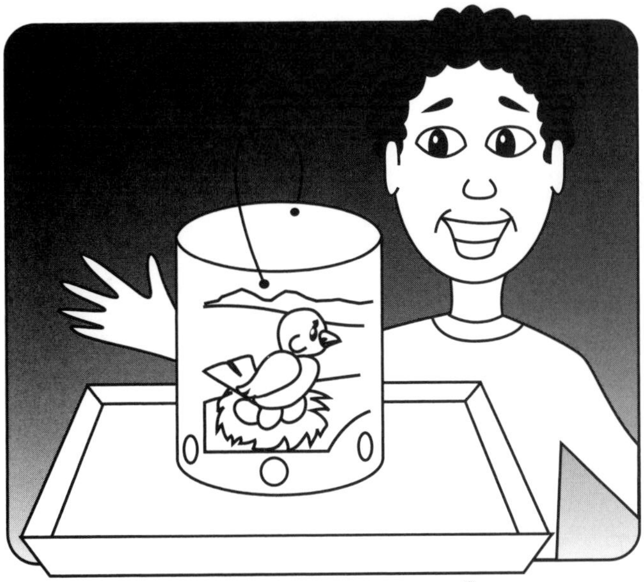

Prayer Thought

I am glad that God loves me even more than little birds.

Memory Verse

Don't be afraid, you are worth more than many sparrows.
~ Luke 12:7

What You Need

- page 14, duplicated
- juice cans
- small foam plates or meat trays
- crayons
- scissors
- tape
- pencils
- yarn
- bird seed

Before Class

Trace the top of the juice can opening on foam, cut out the circle and discard. This will be the feeding tray. (When the tray is slipped over the juice can, the metal ring at the bottom of the can will prevent the tray from falling off.) Also, poke four holes (½" or smaller) at the bottom of the can just above the metal ring. Finally, poke two holes at the top edge for a hanger. Make one per child.

What to Do

1. Instruct the students to color and cut out the strips to cover the cans.
2. Maintain the theme of God's care as the students work. Say, **God loves each of us very much. He tells us in the Bible that He watches over even little birds, and we are worth much more than birds.**
3. Show how to wrap the strips around the cans and tape at the seams.
4. Have the students use pencils to poke holes through the paper to line up with the holes in the bottom and top edges of the cans.
5. Show how to thread yarn through the two holes at the top of the cans and tie to form hangers.
6. Guide the students as they slip the foam trays over the juice cans and down to the bottom edges.
7. The students may fill their bird feeders with seed. The seed will fall through the holes and onto the plate.
8. Close with prayer.

Prayer

God, I know You love Your creation, but You love me even more. Amen.

Bible Lesson

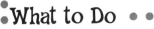

Consider the Lilies
Luke 12:22-34

Prayers for Care

Don't be afraid, you are worth
more than many sparrows.
-Luke 12:7

GOD'S UMBRELLA

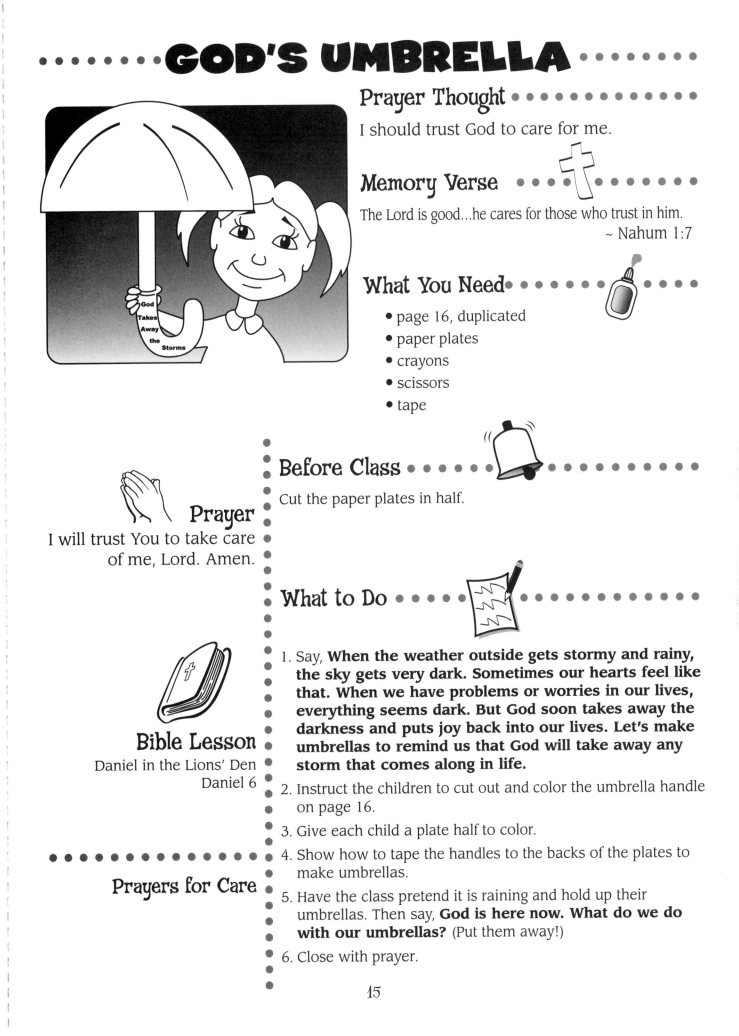

Prayer Thought

I should trust God to care for me.

Memory Verse

The Lord is good...he cares for those who trust in him.
~ Nahum 1:7

What You Need

- page 16, duplicated
- paper plates
- crayons
- scissors
- tape

Before Class

Cut the paper plates in half.

What to Do

1. Say, **When the weather outside gets stormy and rainy, the sky gets very dark. Sometimes our hearts feel like that. When we have problems or worries in our lives, everything seems dark. But God soon takes away the darkness and puts joy back into our lives. Let's make umbrellas to remind us that God will take away any storm that comes along in life.**
2. Instruct the children to cut out and color the umbrella handle on page 16.
3. Give each child a plate half to color.
4. Show how to tape the handles to the backs of the plates to make umbrellas.
5. Have the class pretend it is raining and hold up their umbrellas. Then say, **God is here now. What do we do with our umbrellas?** (Put them away!)
6. Close with prayer.

Prayer

I will trust You to take care of me, Lord. Amen.

Bible Lesson

Daniel in the Lions' Den
Daniel 6

Prayers for Care

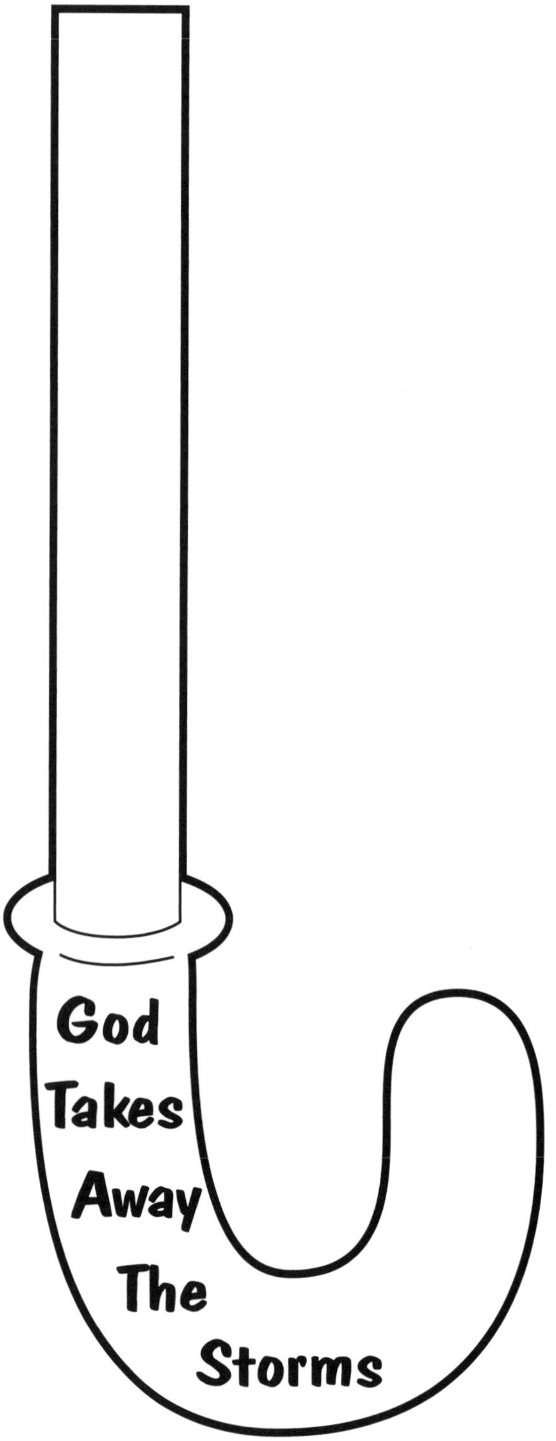
God
Takes
Away
The
Storms

HAPPY FLYERS

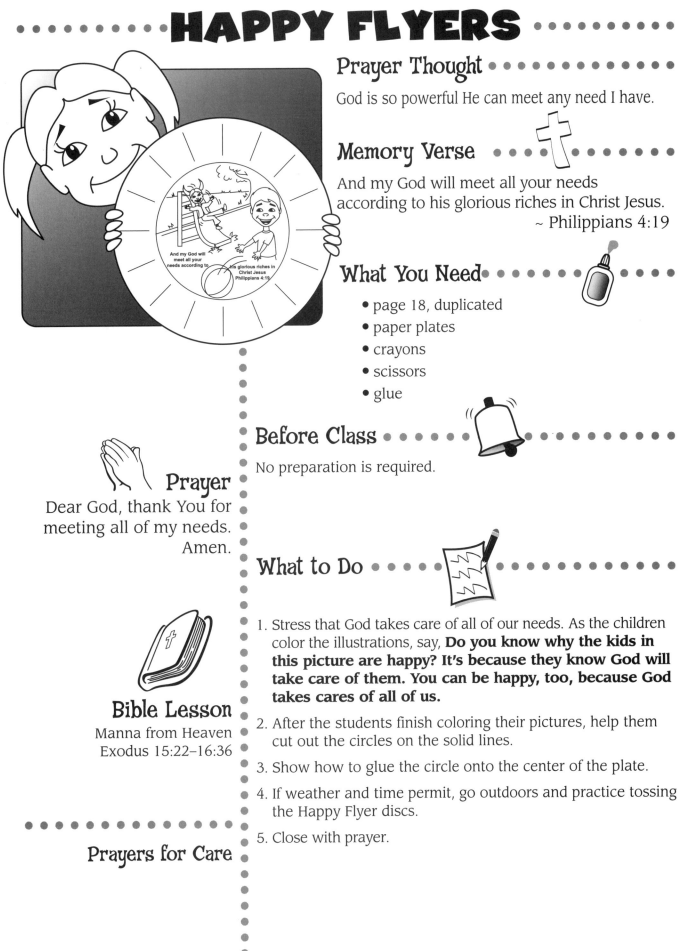

Prayer Thought

God is so powerful He can meet any need I have.

Memory Verse

And my God will meet all your needs according to his glorious riches in Christ Jesus.
~ Philippians 4:19

What You Need

- page 18, duplicated
- paper plates
- crayons
- scissors
- glue

Before Class

No preparation is required.

What to Do

1. Stress that God takes care of all of our needs. As the children color the illustrations, say, **Do you know why the kids in this picture are happy? It's because they know God will take care of them. You can be happy, too, because God takes cares of all of us.**
2. After the students finish coloring their pictures, help them cut out the circles on the solid lines.
3. Show how to glue the circle onto the center of the plate.
4. If weather and time permit, go outdoors and practice tossing the Happy Flyer discs.
5. Close with prayer.

Prayer

Dear God, thank You for meeting all of my needs. Amen.

Bible Lesson

Manna from Heaven
Exodus 15:22–16:36

Prayers for Care

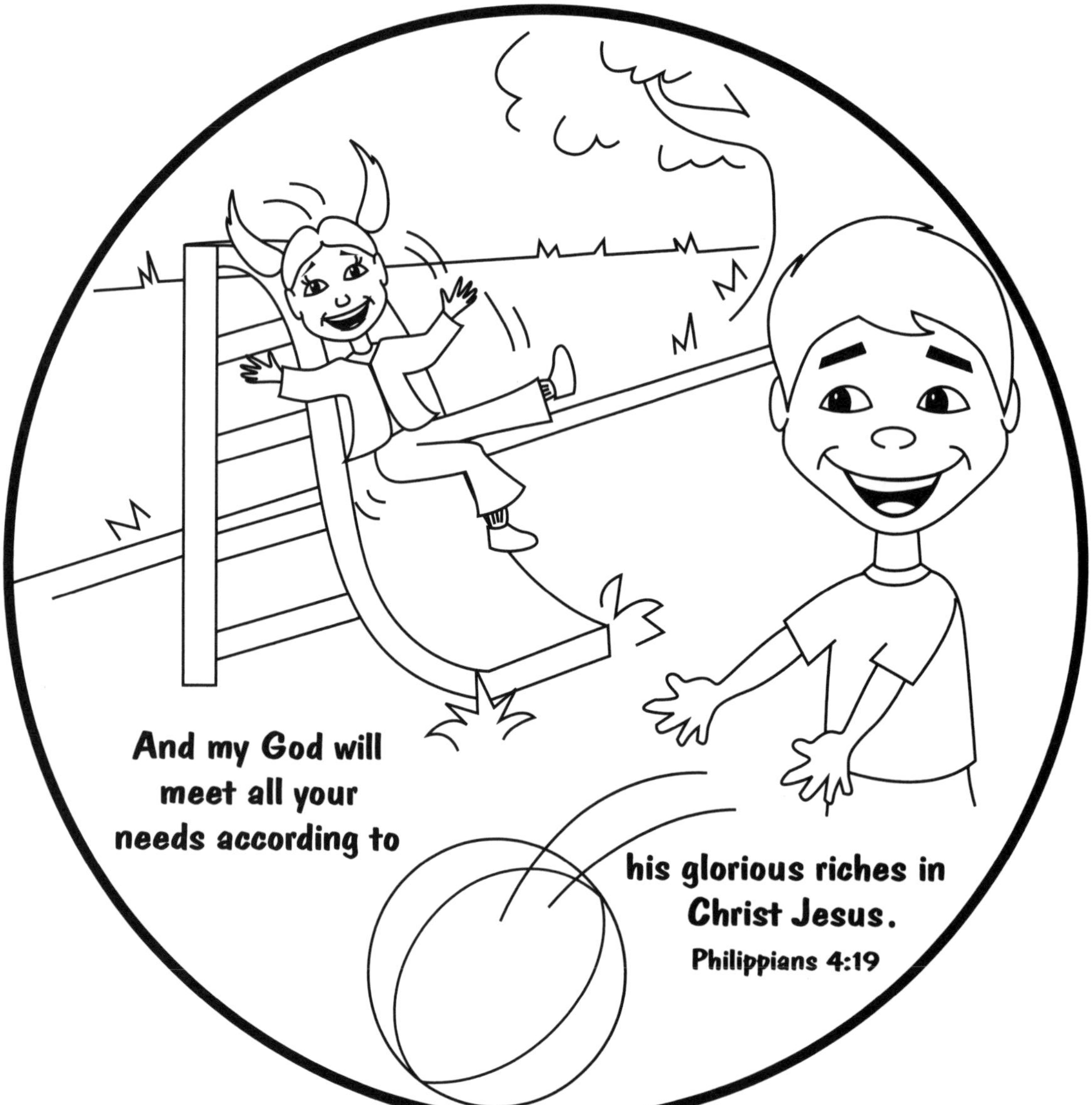
And my God will
meet all your
needs according to
his glorious riches in
Christ Jesus.
Philippians 4:19

JESUS AND CHILDREN RIBBON MOBILE

Prayer Thought

I love Jesus and He loves me.

Memory Verse

Let the little children come to me.
~ Matthew 19:14

What You Need

- page 20, duplicated
- ribbon
- crayons
- scissors
- crayons
- yarn

Before Class

Cut two 10-inch lengths of ribbon for each child. Cut short pieces of yarn to make hangers for each child's mobile.

What to Do

1. Have the children color the figures on the page.
2. Help them cut out the mobile pieces.
3. Show how to tape the two ribbons to the bottom edge of the Jesus figure. Then show how to tape the pictures of children to the ribbons, two on each ribbon.
4. Go around and tape a loop of yarn to the top of each Jesus figure for hanging the mobiles.
5. Say, **Jesus loves children. He called them to Him so He could hug them and tell them how much He loved them. This week when you pray, remember that Jesus loves you. Tell Jesus you love Him, too!**
6. Repeat the prayer thought with the children, then close with prayer.

Prayer

Jesus, I love You very much. I am glad You love little children like me. Amen.

Bible Lesson

Jesus welcomes the children.
Matthew 19:13-15

Prayers for Care

Let the little
children come to me.
Matthew 19:14

JONAH SHAPE BOOK

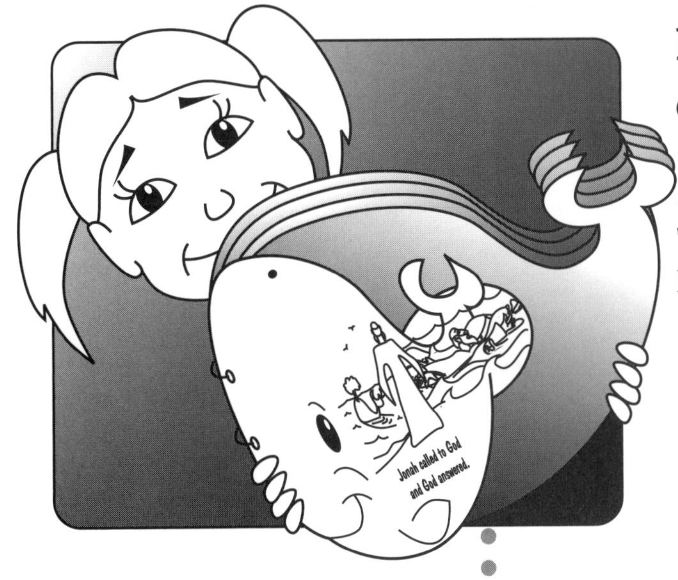

Prayer Thought

God hears and answers my prayers.

Memory Verse

I called to the Lord, and he answered me.
~ Jonah 2:2

What You Need

- page 22, duplicated
- crayons
- white paper
- hole punches
- glue
- yarn

Before Class

Cut out a book cover and use the pattern to cut four extra pages for each child. Cut out the four figures for each child.

What to Do

1. Give each child a book cover, four extra pages and the four story figures.
2. Have the children color the story figures. As they work, say, **Jonah didn't obey God. He ran away on a boat. A big storm scared the men on the boat. Jonah told the men to throw him into the sea and the storm would stop, because he knew God had sent the storm. So they did what he said! Then a big fish swallowed him. Jonah knew God had sent the fish, too. Jonah prayed to God. Soon, the fish spat Jonah onto the shore. He was safe. Jonah said, "I called to the Lord, and You answered me."**
3. Show how to glue one figure on each of the four extra pages.
4. Have the children color the book covers.
5. Show how to put all the pages together, with the cover on top. Go around and punch two holes where indicated on the left side of each book, through all the pages.
6. Help the children thread yarn through the holes and tie it to hold the books together.
7. Say, **Let's talk to God and thank Him for answering our prayers.** Close with prayer.

Prayer

God, You are so good to me. You hear my prayers. You answer my prayers. I love You! Amen.

Bible Lesson

Jonah and the big fish.
Jonah 1–2

Prayers for Care

Jonah called to God
and God answered.

NOAH SPONGE PAINTING

Prayer Thought

God cared for Noah and He cares for me.

Memory Verse

God remembered Noah.
~ Genesis 8:1

What You Need

- page 24, duplicated
- small pieces of sponge
- clothespins
- blue tempera or acrylic paint
- foam plate
- paint smocks

Before Class

You may want to provide paint smocks (men's old shirts work well) to protect clothing from paint.

What to Do

1. As the children color the pictures of the ark, stress how God took care of all who were inside the ark. Say, **Have you ever stayed indoors during a rainy day? Can you imagine what it would be like to stay in for a whole month? Noah was inside with all of those animals for 40 days! Who do you think took care of all of Noah's needs while he was in the ark? Isn't it wonderful that our God will take care of us no matter what situation we are in?**
2. Pour a thin layer of paint onto the foam plate.
3. Give each child a piece of sponge clipped to a clothespin.
4. Guide them as they dip the sponges into the paint, then blot it onto the pictures to make flood waters.
5. Practice the memory verse with the class.
6. Close with prayer.

Prayer

God, You proved You care for us by watching over Noah. Thank You. Amen.

Bible Lesson

Noah and the Ark
Genesis 6–9

Prayers for Care

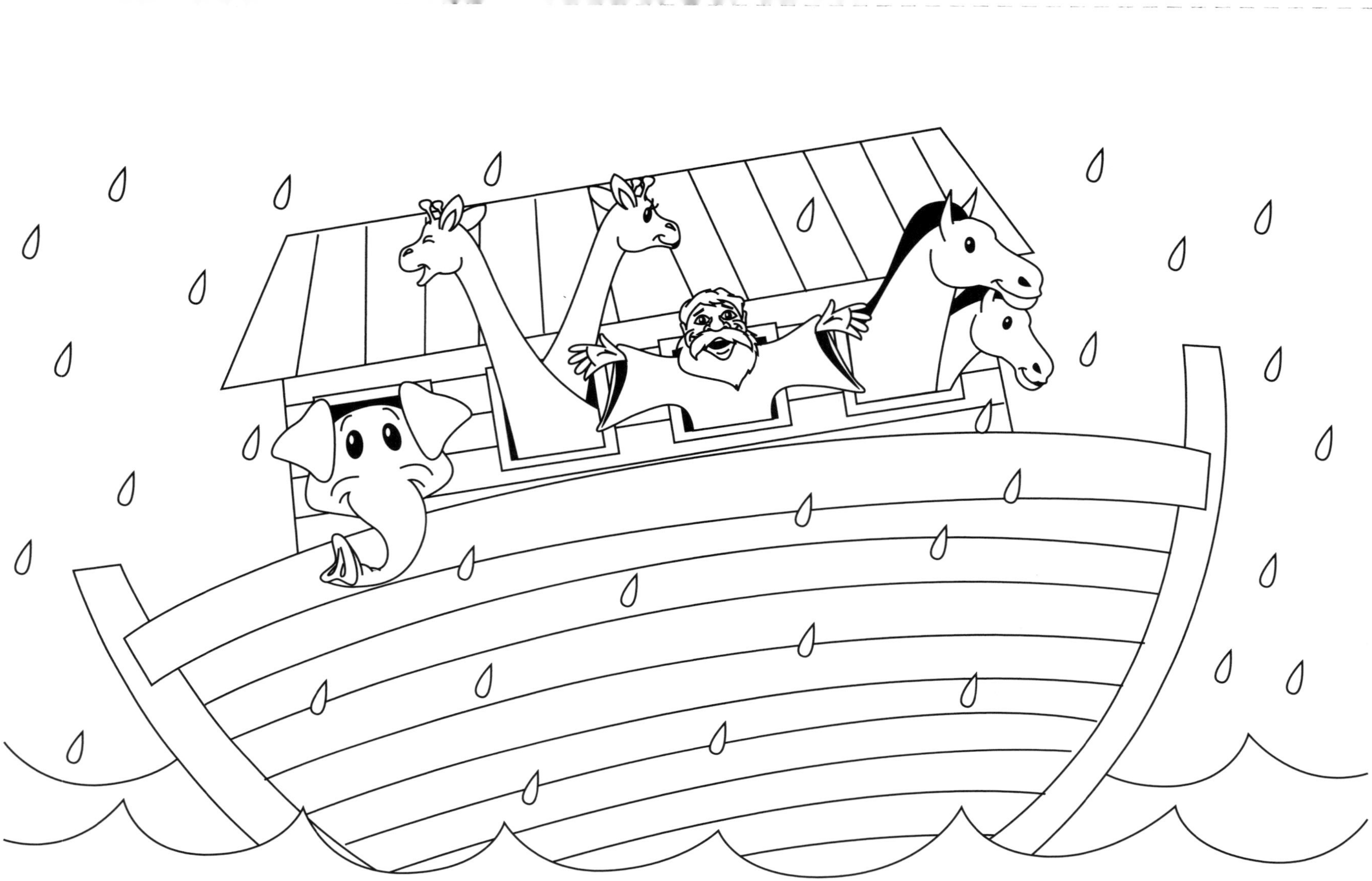

God remembered Noah.

Genesis 8:1

FUZZY SHEEP PLAQUE

Psalm 23
A psalm of David. The Lord is my shepherd, I shall not be in want. He makes me lie down in green pastures, he leads me beside quiet waters, he restores my soul. He guides me in paths of righteousness for his name's sake. Even though I walk through the valley of the shadow of death, I will fear no evil, for you are with me; your rod and your staff, they comfort me. You prepare a table before me in the presence of my enemies. You anoint my head with oil; my cup overflows. Surely goodness and love will follow me all the days of my life, and I will dwell in the house of the Lord forever.

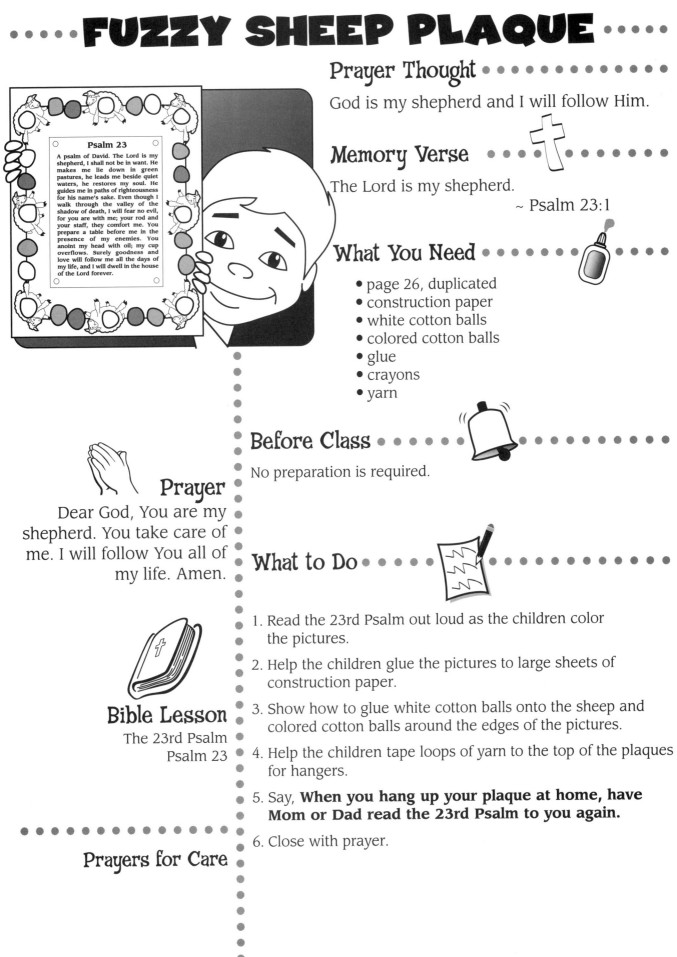

Prayer Thought

God is my shepherd and I will follow Him.

Memory Verse

The Lord is my shepherd.
~ Psalm 23:1

What You Need

- page 26, duplicated
- construction paper
- white cotton balls
- colored cotton balls
- glue
- crayons
- yarn

Before Class

No preparation is required.

Prayer

Dear God, You are my shepherd. You take care of me. I will follow You all of my life. Amen.

What to Do

1. Read the 23rd Psalm out loud as the children color the pictures.
2. Help the children glue the pictures to large sheets of construction paper.
3. Show how to glue white cotton balls onto the sheep and colored cotton balls around the edges of the pictures.
4. Help the children tape loops of yarn to the top of the plaques for hangers.
5. Say, **When you hang up your plaque at home, have Mom or Dad read the 23rd Psalm to you again.**
6. Close with prayer.

Bible Lesson

The 23rd Psalm
Psalm 23

Prayers for Care

Psalm 23

A psalm of David. The Lord is my shepherd, I shall not be in want. He makes me lie down in green pastures, he leads me beside quiet waters, he restores my soul. He guides me in paths of righteousness for his name's sake. Even though I walk through the valley of the shadow of death, I will fear no evil, for you are with me; your rod and your staff, they comfort me. You prepare a table before me in the presence of my enemies. You anoint my head with oil; my cup overflows. Surely goodness and love will follow me all the days of my life, and I will dwell in the house of the Lord forever.

TRUST 'N' TIE BOOKMARK

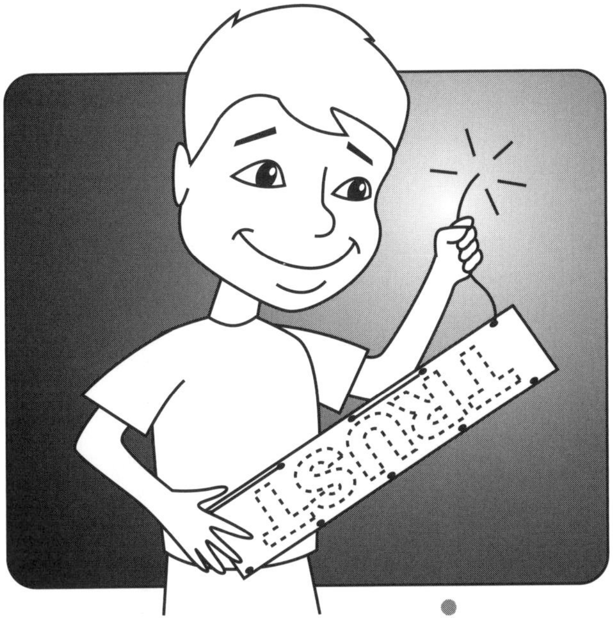

Prayer Thought

I will not be afraid because I trust God to take care of me.

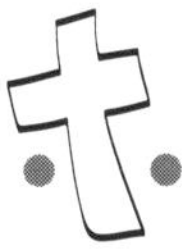

Memory Verse

I will trust and not be afraid. The Lord is my strength.
~ Isaiah 12:2

What You Need

- page 28, duplicated
- crayons
- scissors
- yarn
- hole punch
- tape

Before Class

Cut out the bookmarks from page 28 and use a hole punch to make holes for yarn. Cut a 22" length of yarn for each child and knot each piece at one end. Place a small piece of tape around one end of each piece of yarn so it will lace through the holes more easily.

What to Do

1. Guide the students as they trace the words TRUST and GOD with crayons on the bookmarks.
2. As they color their bookmarks, practice the memory verse with the class.
3. Show how to place the two bookmarks back-to-back.
4. Have them color the pictures of Jesus and the disciples.
5. Help the students hold both pieces together and, starting at the bottom right, lace the yarn through the holes, ending at the bottom left. Tie.
6. Tell the students that they should place their bookmarks in their Bibles or Bible story books at home so they will know which parts of the book they have "read."
7. Close with prayer.

Prayer

You are my strength, God, so I will trust You and not be afraid. Amen.

Bible Lesson

Moses Crosses the Red Sea
Exodus 13:17–14:31

Prayers for Care

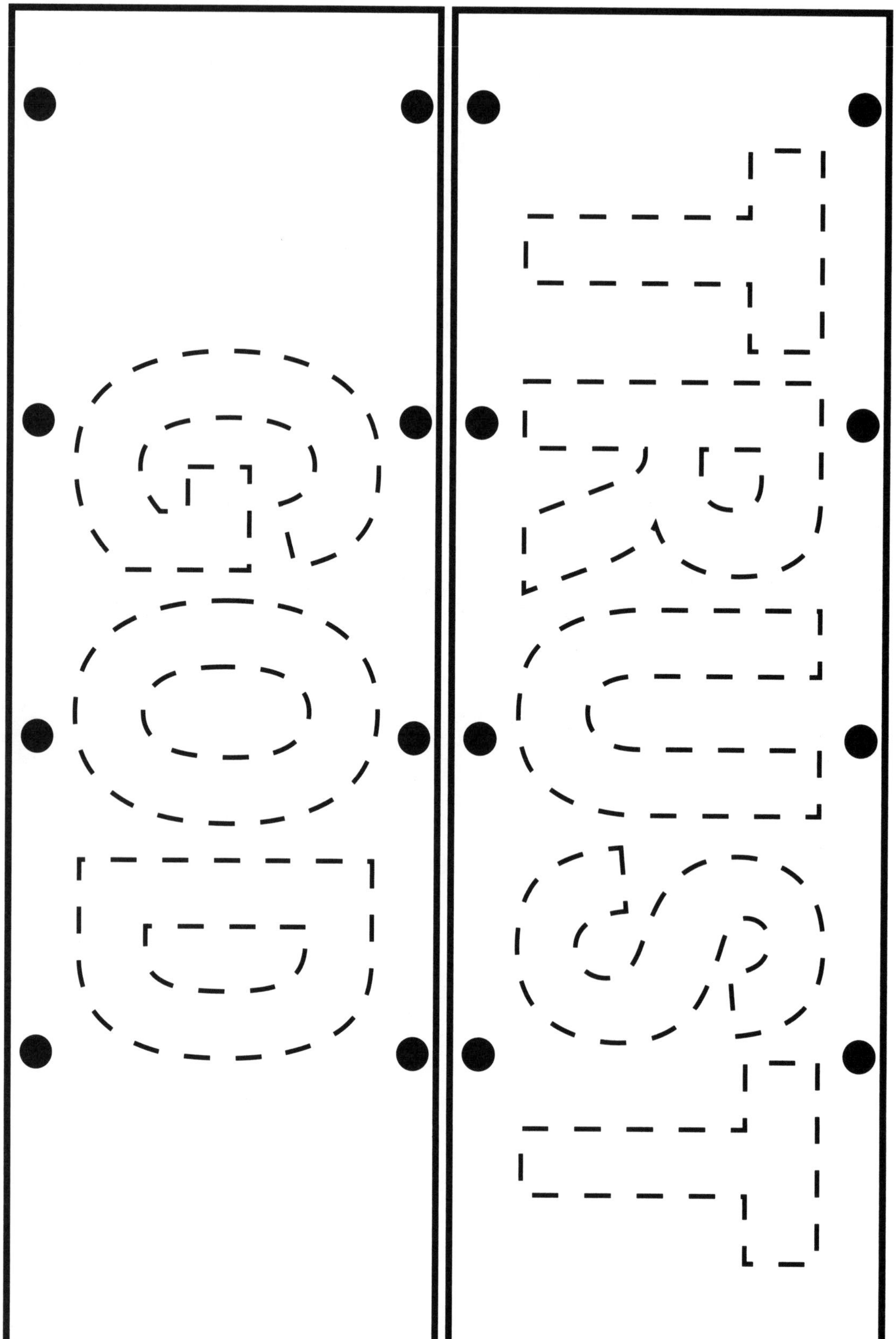
GOD
TRUST

EARS TO LISTEN TO GOD

Prayer Thought

I will listen to and obey God's Word.

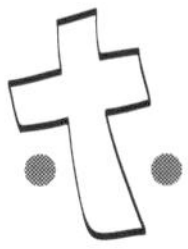

Memory Verse

Blessed are those who hear the word of God and obey it.

~ Luke 11:28

What You Need

- page 30, duplicated
- crayons

Prayer

Dear God, help me to keep doing what is right. Amen.

Before Class

No preparation is required.

What to Do

1. As the children color page 30, help them read the poem.
2. Repeat the memory verse with the class.
3. Ask, **Where can we hear God's Word? What kinds of things does God tell us to do? Why is it important that we do what God says?**
4. Close with prayer.

Bible Lesson

Jonah and the Whale
The book of Jonah

Prayers of Commitment

My ears can hear a pretty bird singing.
My ears can hear a church bell ringing.
My ears can hear my mother call.
But hearing God's Word is the best thing of all.

Blessed are those who hear the word of God and obey it.
Luke 11:28

FIND THE GOOD FOOD

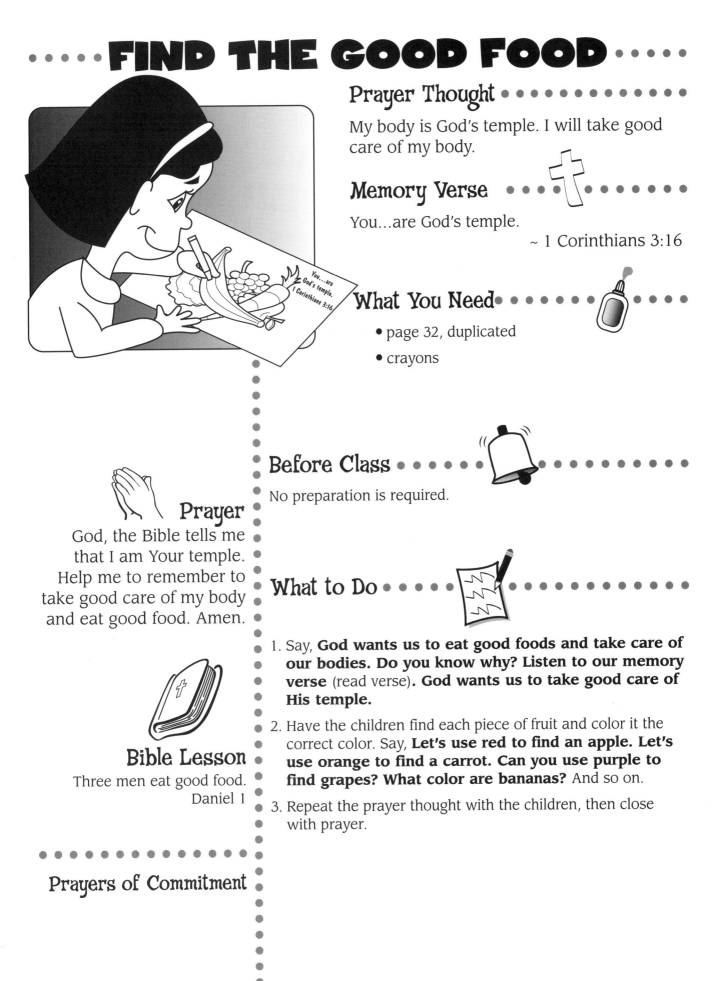

Prayer Thought

My body is God's temple. I will take good care of my body.

Memory Verse

You...are God's temple.

~ 1 Corinthians 3:16

What You Need

- page 32, duplicated
- crayons

Before Class

No preparation is required.

What to Do

1. Say, **God wants us to eat good foods and take care of our bodies. Do you know why? Listen to our memory verse** (read verse)**. God wants us to take good care of His temple.**
2. Have the children find each piece of fruit and color it the correct color. Say, **Let's use red to find an apple. Let's use orange to find a carrot. Can you use purple to find grapes? What color are bananas?** And so on.
3. Repeat the prayer thought with the children, then close with prayer.

Prayer

God, the Bible tells me that I am Your temple. Help me to remember to take good care of my body and eat good food. Amen.

Bible Lesson

Three men eat good food.
Daniel 1

Prayers of Commitment

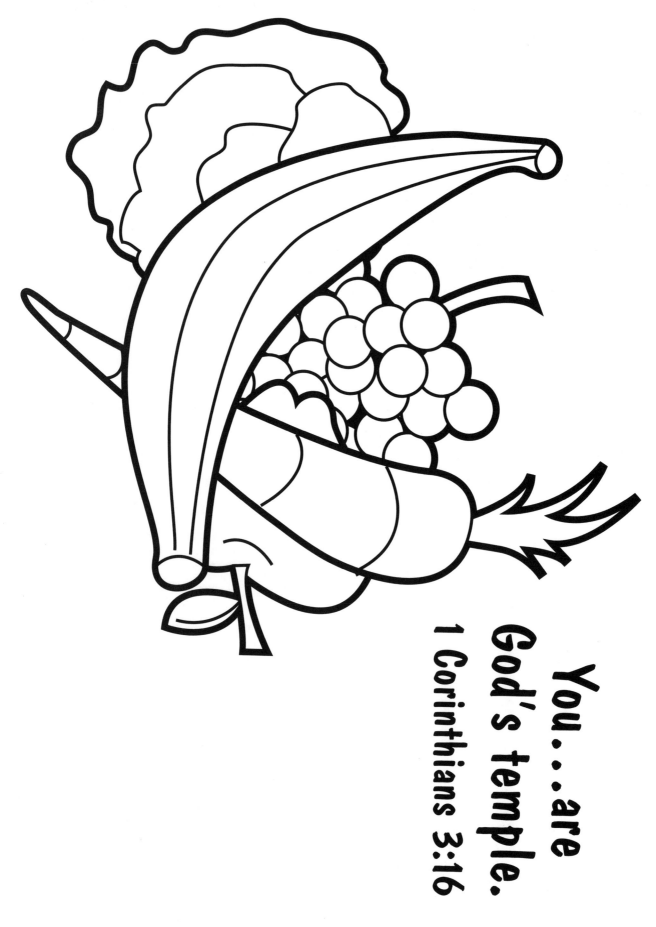

You...are
God's temple.
1 Corinthians 3:16

FOLLOW JESUS WINDSOCK

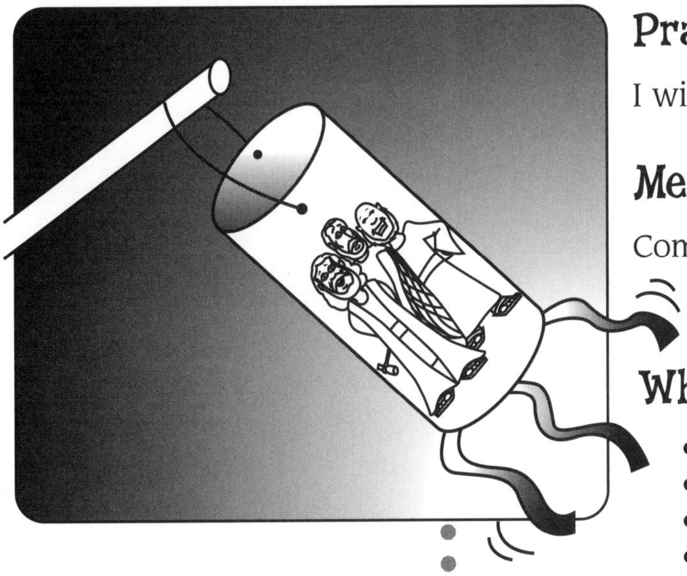

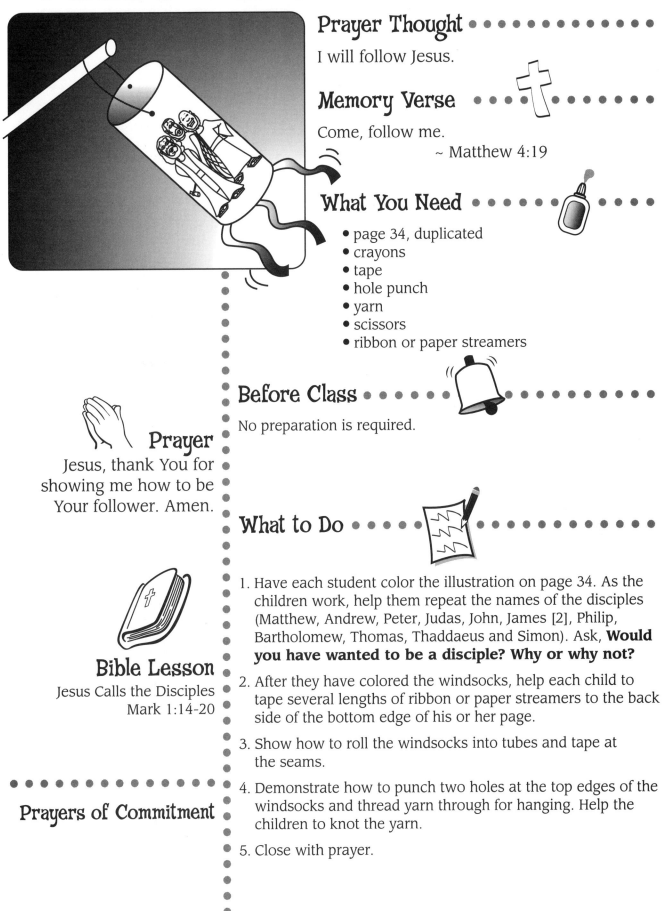

Prayer Thought

I will follow Jesus.

Memory Verse

Come, follow me.

~ Matthew 4:19

What You Need

- page 34, duplicated
- crayons
- tape
- hole punch
- yarn
- scissors
- ribbon or paper streamers

Before Class

No preparation is required.

What to Do

1. Have each student color the illustration on page 34. As the children work, help them repeat the names of the disciples (Matthew, Andrew, Peter, Judas, John, James [2], Philip, Bartholomew, Thomas, Thaddaeus and Simon). Ask, **Would you have wanted to be a disciple? Why or why not?**
2. After they have colored the windsocks, help each child to tape several lengths of ribbon or paper streamers to the back side of the bottom edge of his or her page.
3. Show how to roll the windsocks into tubes and tape at the seams.
4. Demonstrate how to punch two holes at the top edges of the windsocks and thread yarn through for hanging. Help the children to knot the yarn.
5. Close with prayer.

Prayer

Jesus, thank You for showing me how to be Your follower. Amen.

Bible Lesson

Jesus Calls the Disciples
Mark 1:14-20

Prayers of Commitment

Come, follow me.

Matthew 4:19

GENTLE BUBBLES

Prayer Thought

I will be gentle and patient.

Memory Verse

Be completely humble and gentle; be patient, bearing with one another in love.

~ Ephesians 4:2

What You Need

- page 36, duplicated (if desired)
- chenille stems
- bubble solution
- bowls

Before Class

Prepare the bubble solution and pour some into a bowl for each group of children. If desired, duplicate page 36 to show shapes for forming wands.

What to Do

1. Talk about gentleness and patience. As the children form bubble wands from chenille stems (either freehand or by forming shapes as shown on page 36), ask them to give you examples of how they can be gentle and patient.
2. Blow a bubble in the classroom and discuss how to blow gently to avoid destroying the bubble on the wand.
3. Talk about patience and taking turns. Explain how more than one person can share a dish of bubble solution.
4. Take the class outdoors to blow bubbles. Ask, **Is it easy to be gentle and patient?**
5. Close with prayer.

Prayer

God, help me to show Your love by being gentle and patient with others. Amen.

Bible Lesson

Doing Good to All
Galatians 6:1-10

Prayers of Commitment

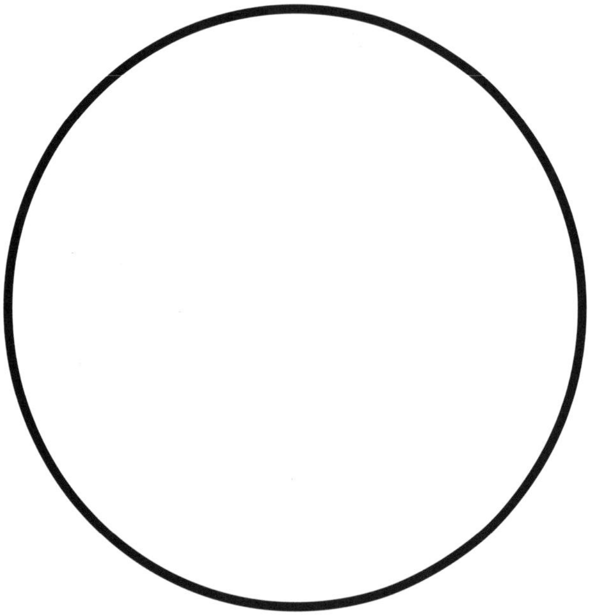

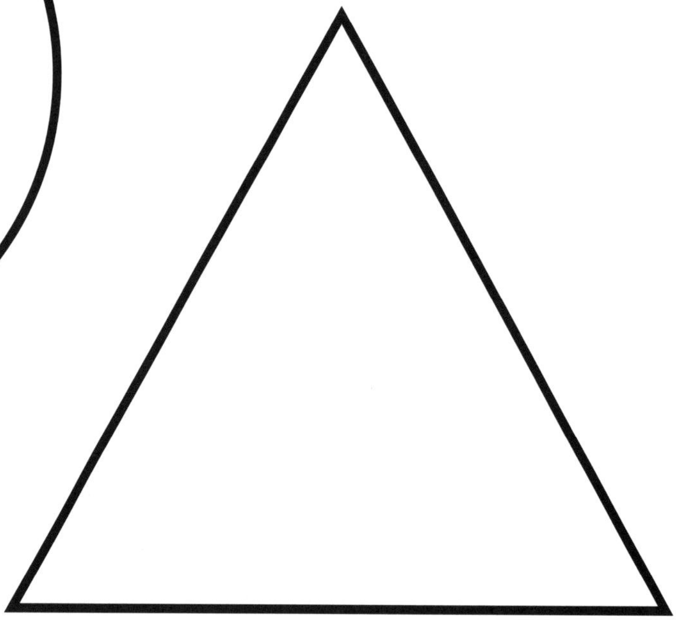

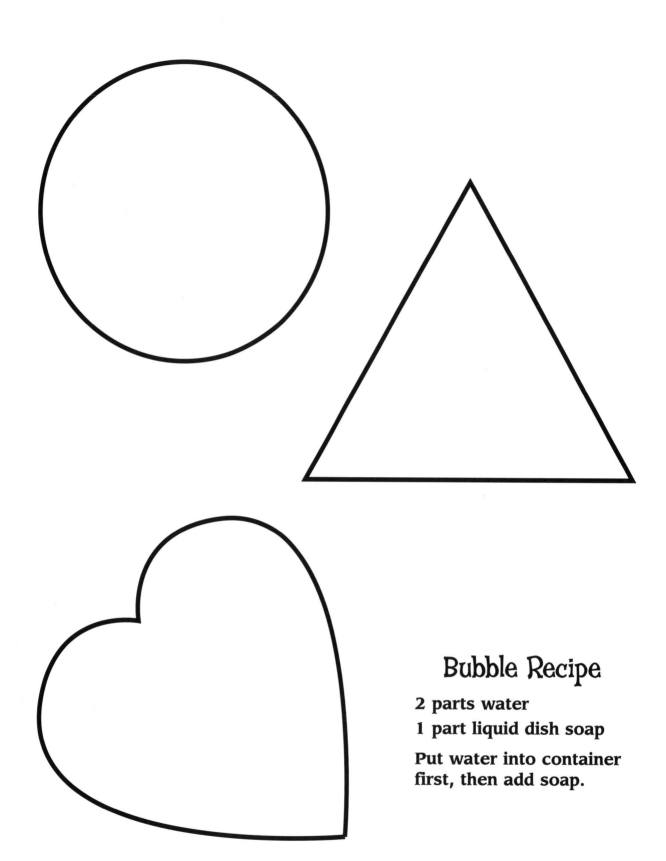

Bubble Recipe

2 parts water

1 part liquid dish soap

Put water into container first, then add soap.

HELPER MAGNETS

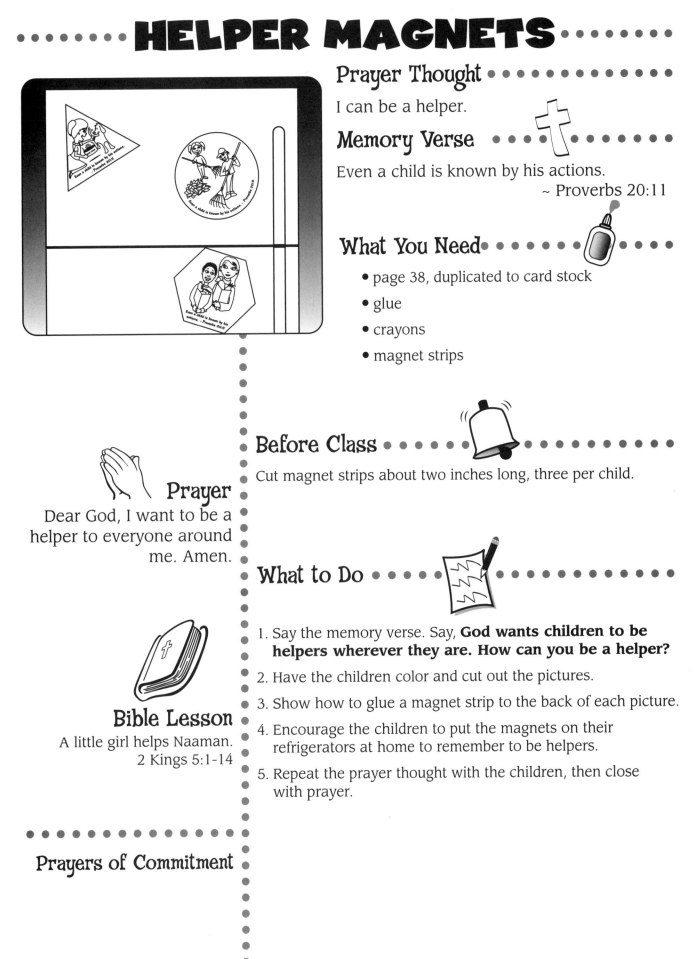

Prayer Thought

I can be a helper.

Memory Verse

Even a child is known by his actions.
~ Proverbs 20:11

What You Need

- page 38, duplicated to card stock
- glue
- crayons
- magnet strips

Before Class

Cut magnet strips about two inches long, three per child.

What to Do

1. Say the memory verse. Say, **God wants children to be helpers wherever they are. How can you be a helper?**
2. Have the children color and cut out the pictures.
3. Show how to glue a magnet strip to the back of each picture.
4. Encourage the children to put the magnets on their refrigerators at home to remember to be helpers.
5. Repeat the prayer thought with the children, then close with prayer.

Prayer

Dear God, I want to be a helper to everyone around me. Amen.

Bible Lesson

A little girl helps Naaman.
2 Kings 5:1-14

Prayers of Commitment

DOG FOOD
Even a child is known by his actions.
- Proverbs 20:11

Even a child is known by his
actions. - Proverbs 20:11

Even a child is known by his actions. - Proverbs 20:11

MISSIONS SHOE BANK

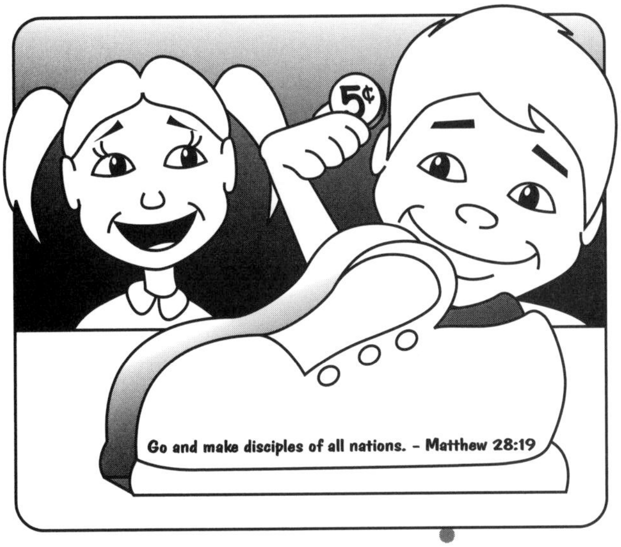

5¢
Go and make disciples of all nations. - Matthew 28:19

Prayer Thought

I will help to take the Good News all over the world.

Memory Verse

Go and make disciples of all nations.
~ Matthew 28:19

What You Need

- page 40, duplicated
- crayons
- scissors
- yarn
- hole punch
- small pudding mix boxes
- glue

Before Class

If desired, cut a slit in one end of each box before class.

What to Do

1. Talk about one of your church's missions as the children color the shoes on page 40. Ask, **Do you know what a missionary is? Missionaries go all over the world and teach people about Jesus. Our church has missionaries in** (name country or region)**. Let's make banks so we can save some money to give to these missionaries.**
2. Guide the children as they cut out the shoes on the outer solid lines, then fold the shoes on the dashed lines.
3. Demonstrate how to set the box inside the shoes, with the coin slits facing up. Have them glue the boxes at the bottom.
4. Show how to glue the sides of the shoes to the boxes.
5. Tell the children that their shoe banks will remind them to collect money for missionaries, who travel to spread the Good News.
6. Close with prayer for missionaries.

Prayer

I will pray every day that people all over the world will learn about You. Amen.

Bible Lesson

The Great Commission
Matthew 28:16-20

Prayers of Commitment

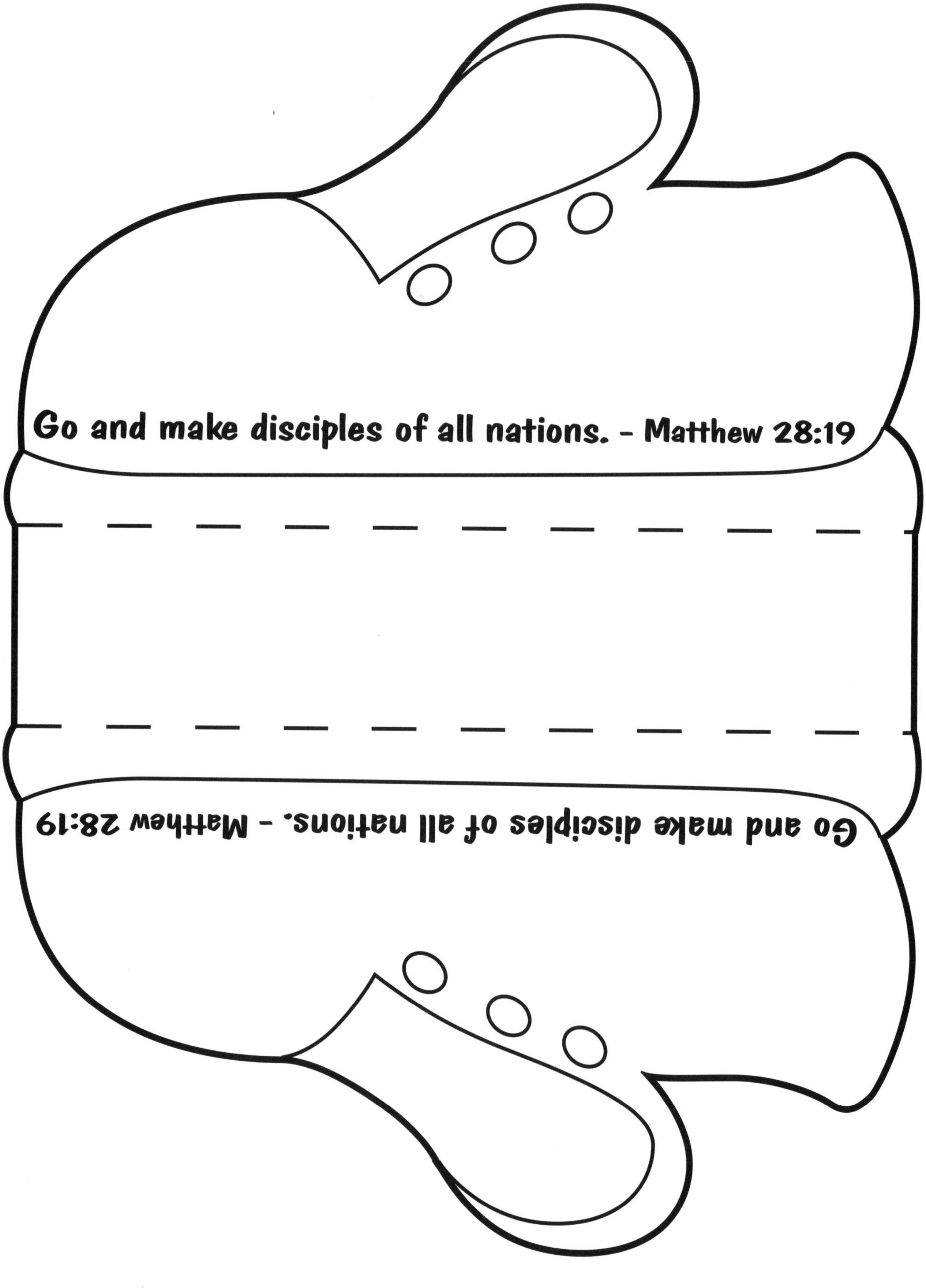
Go and make disciples of all nations. - Matthew 28:19
Go and make disciples of all nations. - Matthew 28:19

PRAYER POSTER

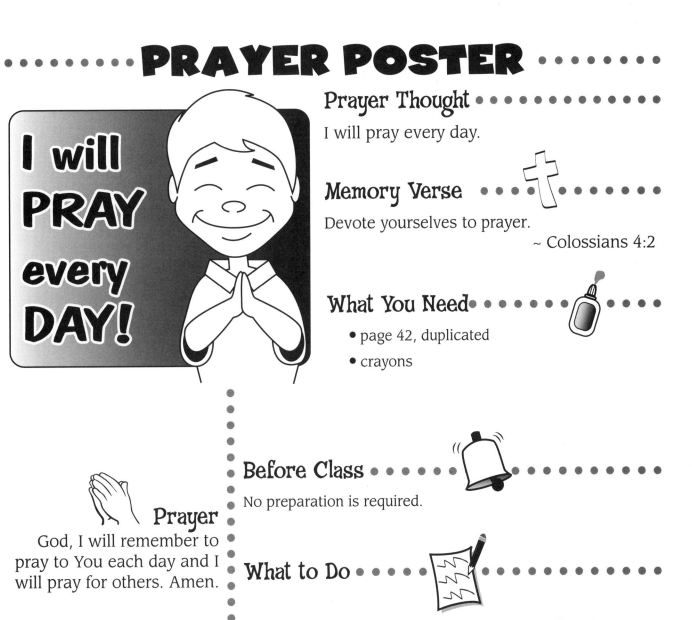

Prayer Thought

I will pray every day.

Memory Verse

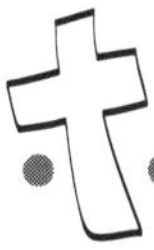

Devote yourselves to prayer.

~ Colossians 4:2

What You Need

- page 42, duplicated
- crayons

Prayer

God, I will remember to pray to You each day and I will pray for others. Amen.

Bible Lesson

The Parable of the Persistent Widow
Luke 18:1-8

Prayers of Commitment

Before Class

No preparation is required.

What to Do

1. Distribute one sheet per child, but wait to pass out the crayons.
2. Ask a child to pray for the class.
3. Distribute the crayons, then tell the class that they are to color only the square for "Sunday" (or whichever day it is). Explain that everyone is to take a prayer poster home and color a square on each day after praying.
4. Encourage the children to bring their completed posters back the following week. Display the posters on your classroom bulletin board. Consider offering a small prize for all who return their posters completed.
5. Close with a prayer for devotion.

Sunday
Monday
Tuesday
Wednesday
Thursday
Friday
Saturday
I will PRAY EVERY DAY!

ROCKING SHEEP

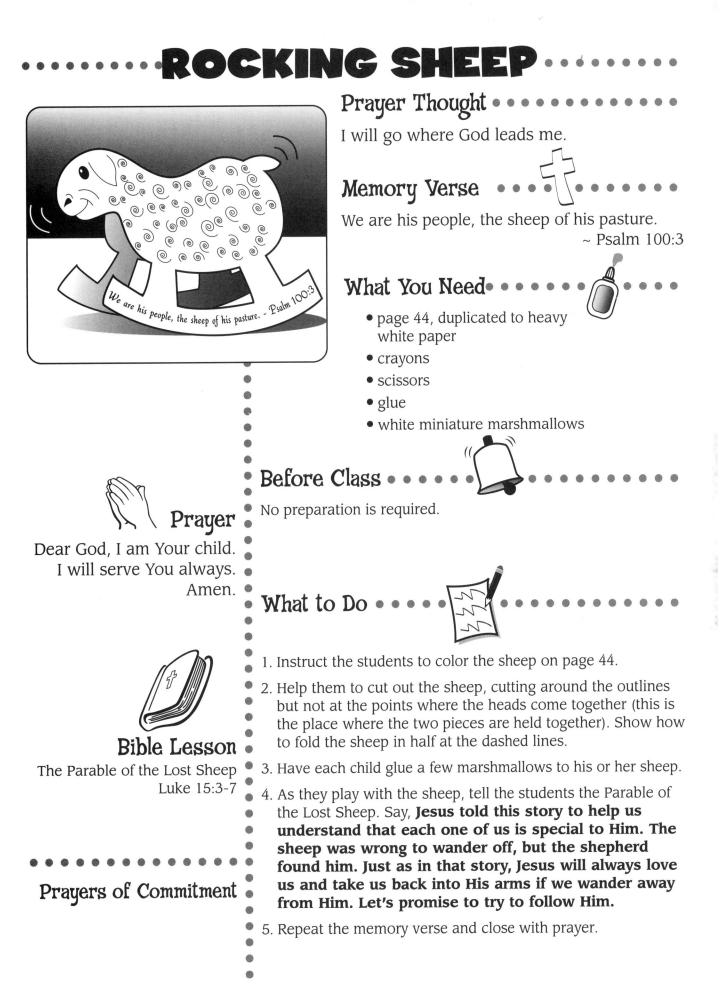

Prayer Thought

I will go where God leads me.

Memory Verse

We are his people, the sheep of his pasture.

~ Psalm 100:3

What You Need

- page 44, duplicated to heavy white paper
- crayons
- scissors
- glue
- white miniature marshmallows

Before Class

No preparation is required.

What to Do

1. Instruct the students to color the sheep on page 44.
2. Help them to cut out the sheep, cutting around the outlines but not at the points where the heads come together (this is the place where the two pieces are held together). Show how to fold the sheep in half at the dashed lines.
3. Have each child glue a few marshmallows to his or her sheep.
4. As they play with the sheep, tell the students the Parable of the Lost Sheep. Say, **Jesus told this story to help us understand that each one of us is special to Him. The sheep was wrong to wander off, but the shepherd found him. Just as in that story, Jesus will always love us and take us back into His arms if we wander away from Him. Let's promise to try to follow Him.**
5. Repeat the memory verse and close with prayer.

Prayer

Dear God, I am Your child. I will serve You always. Amen.

Bible Lesson

The Parable of the Lost Sheep
Luke 15:3-7

Prayers of Commitment

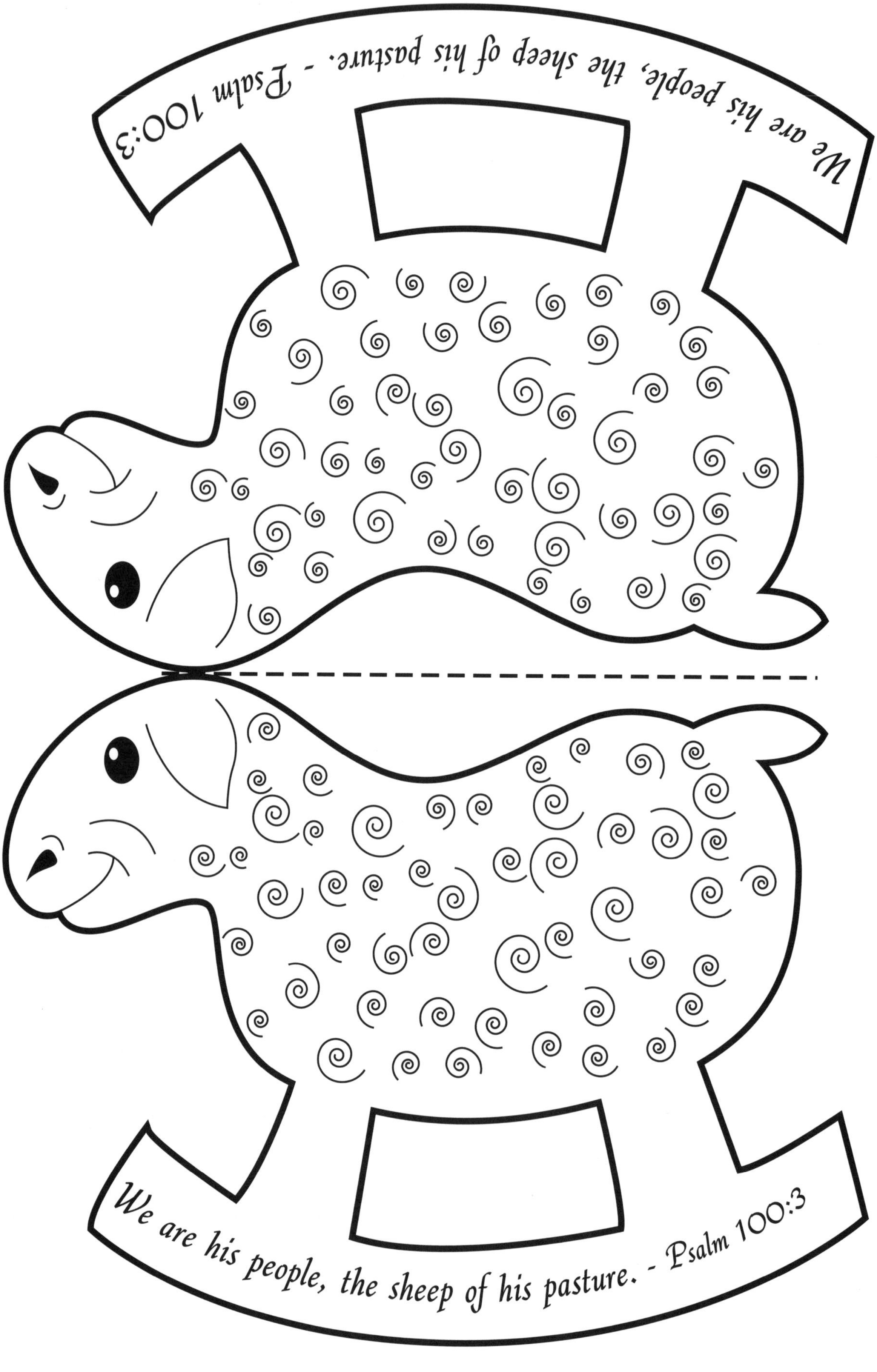
We are his people, the sheep of his pasture. - Psalm 100:3
We are his people, the sheep of his pasture. - Psalm 100:3

WALKING IN LOVE

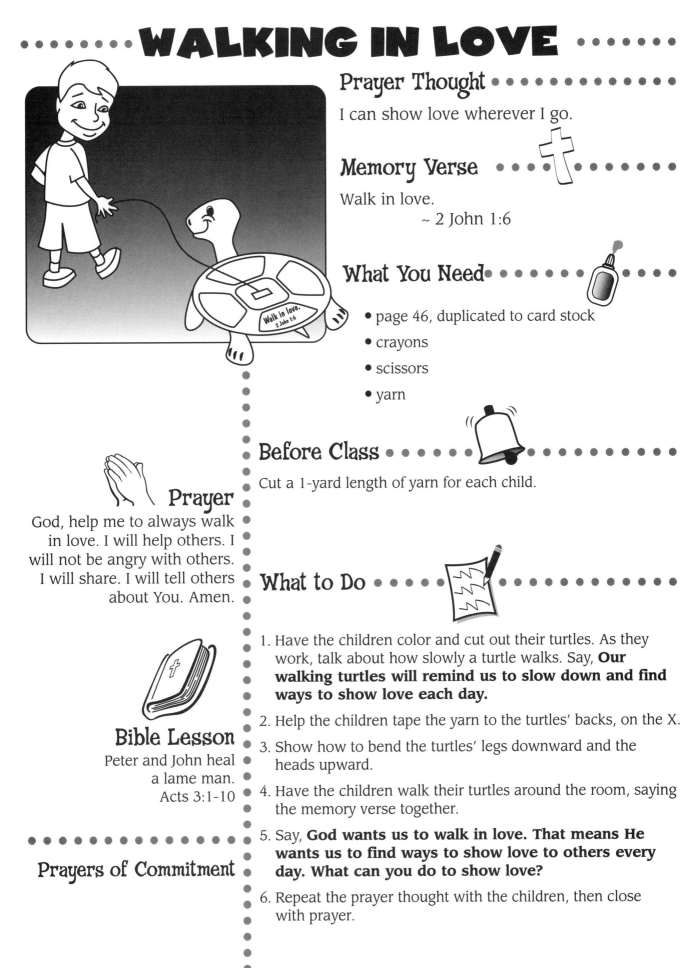

Prayer Thought

I can show love wherever I go.

Memory Verse

Walk in love.

~ 2 John 1:6

What You Need

- page 46, duplicated to card stock
- crayons
- scissors
- yarn

Prayer

God, help me to always walk in love. I will help others. I will not be angry with others. I will share. I will tell others about You. Amen.

Bible Lesson

Peter and John heal a lame man.
Acts 3:1-10

Prayers of Commitment

Before Class

Cut a 1-yard length of yarn for each child.

What to Do

1. Have the children color and cut out their turtles. As they work, talk about how slowly a turtle walks. Say, **Our walking turtles will remind us to slow down and find ways to show love each day.**
2. Help the children tape the yarn to the turtles' backs, on the X.
3. Show how to bend the turtles' legs downward and the heads upward.
4. Have the children walk their turtles around the room, saying the memory verse together.
5. Say, **God wants us to walk in love. That means He wants us to find ways to show love to others every day. What can you do to show love?**
6. Repeat the prayer thought with the children, then close with prayer.

Walk in love.
2 John 1:6

WORSHIP GOD NAPKIN RINGS

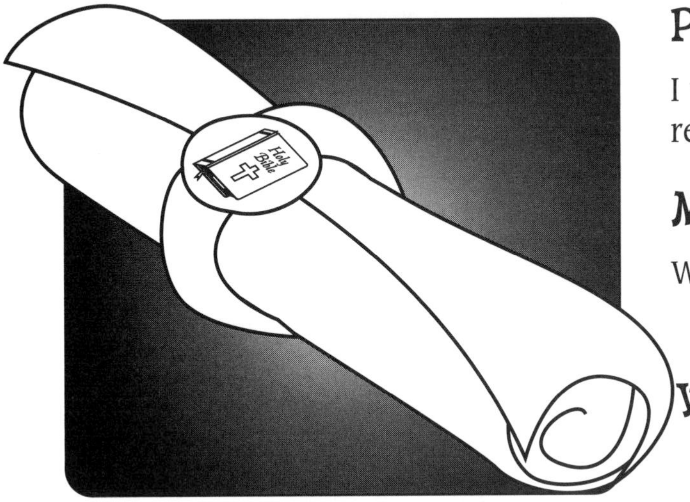

Prayer Thought

I will worship God by going to church, reading my Bible and praying.

Memory Verse

Worship God!
~ Revelation 22:9

What You Need

- page 48, duplicated
- crayons
- scissors
- tape
- paper napkins

Before Class

No preparation is required.

What to Do

1. Have the class cut out the napkin ring strips from page 48.
2. As the students color the strips, talk about the items in the pictures. Say, **Worship God! That's what our Bible says. How do you think we can use the items in the pictures to worship God? Is going to church a way to worship? How about reading our Bibles? Is praying a kind of worship?**
3. Ask the class to repeat the memory verse with you several times.
4. Assist the children with rolling and taping the rings. Let each student fold three napkins and place one in each napkin ring.
5. Close with prayer.

Prayer

God, help me to serve You by worshipping, reading my Bible and praying. Amen.

Bible Lesson

Young Jesus visits God's House
Luke 2:41-52

Prayers of Commitment

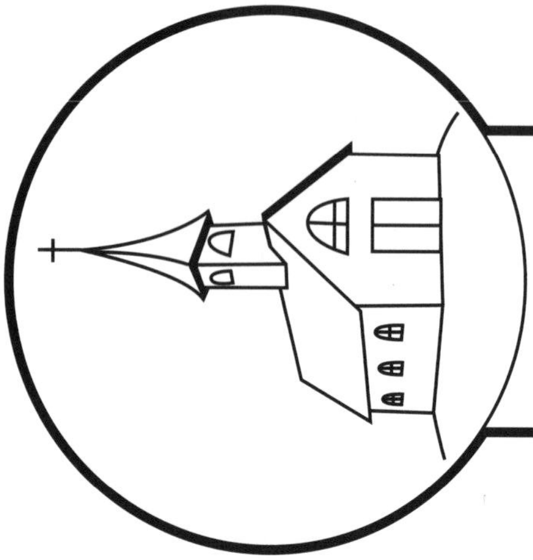

Worship God! - Revelation 22:9

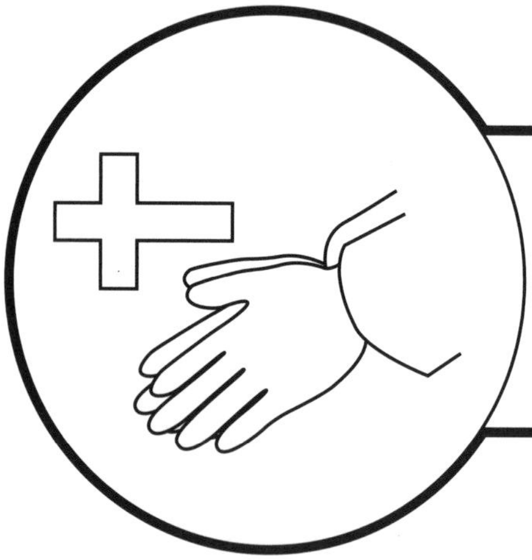

Worship God! - Revelation 22:9

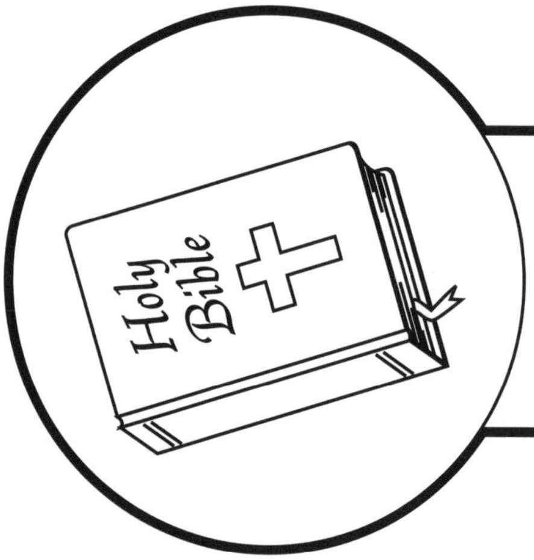

Worship God! - Revelation 22:9

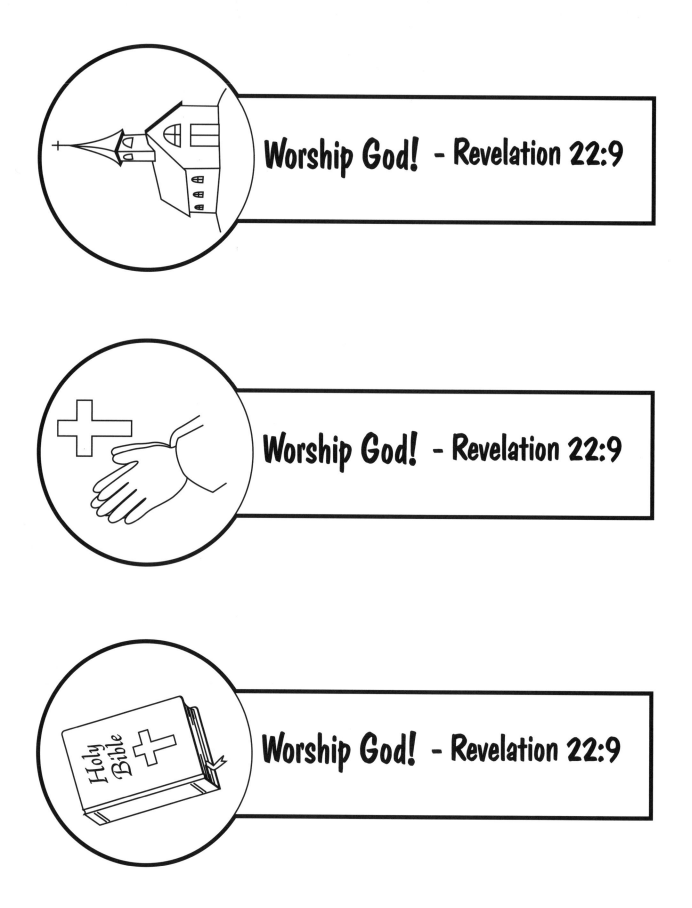

WORSHIP PICTURE PUZZLE

Prayer Thought

I love to go to God's House and worship Him.

Memory Verse

Worship the Lord your God.

~ Luke 4:8

What You Need

- page 50, duplicated
- crayons

Before Class

No preparation is required.

What to Do

1. Guide the children as they circle the items that are used to worship God. Discuss each picture that is circled. Ask, **Can you find the pictures of things we would use to worship God? Draw a circle around the things we use to worship. Who stands by the pulpit? What do we put in this plate? What is this book?**
2. Optional: You might want to have some worship items on hand for the children to see and discuss such as a Bible, an offering tray, a cross, a picture of Jesus, a hymnal or some communion supplies.
3. Repeat the prayer thought with the children, and close with prayer.

Prayer

God, I love to go to Your house. I love to sing, praise and pray to You. I love to give my offerings to help others. Amen.

Bible Lesson

Jesus is tempted.
Luke 4:1-13

Prayers of Commitment

Holy
Bible

CREATION STRAW SIPPERS

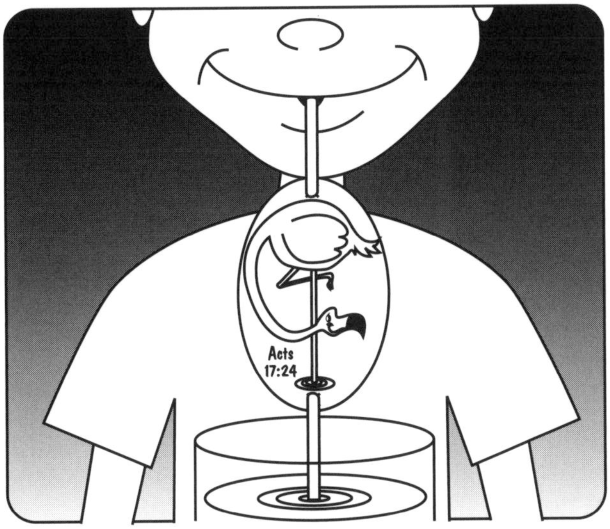

Prayer Thought

I love God's creation.

Memory Verse

God...made the world and everything in it.
~ Acts 17:24

What You Need

- page 52, duplicated
- crayons
- scissors
- plastic drinking straws

Prayer

God, You made a wonderful world. I love the animals, flowers and trees. I love the moon and stars. You are so awesome. I love You. Amen.

Bible Lesson

God will bless His people and all creation.
Ezekiel 38:8-12

Prayers of Praise

Before Class

For younger children, you may want to cut out the figures and make the holes for the straws.

What to Do

1. As the children color and cut out the four creatures, discuss how unique and wonderful each creature is. Ask, **Isn't it fun to watch the creatures that God made? What is your favorite animal** (bug, bird, water creature)**?**
2. Help students cut out the X's on each creature and slip straws through so the creatures show on the outside.
3. Say, **Your Straw Sippers will remind you that God made many interesting creatures for us to enjoy. Let's bow our heads and thank God for His wonderful world.**
4. Close with prayer.

Acts
17:24

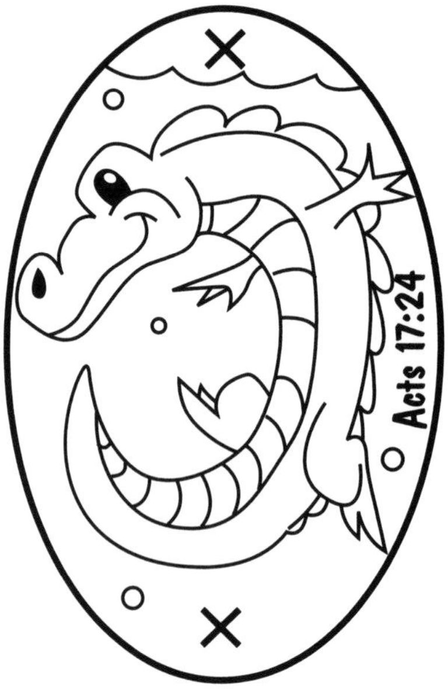
Acts 17:24

Acts
17:24

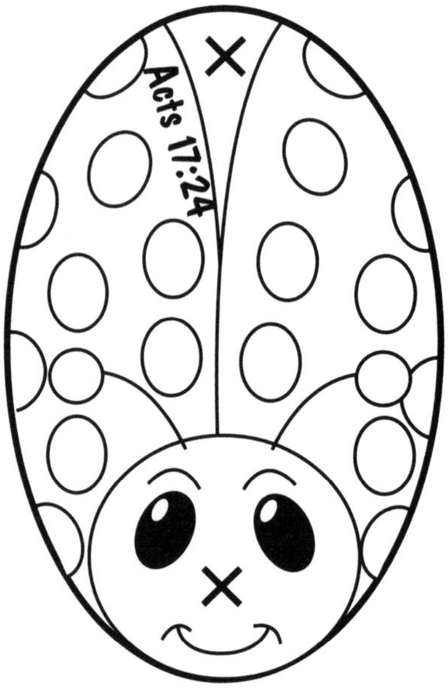
Acts 17:24

EASTER GARLAND

Prayer Thought

I celebrate Easter because Jesus has risen!

Memory Verse

He has risen!
~ Mark 16:6

What You Need

- page 54, duplicated
- yarn
- scissors
- glue
- crayons

Before Class

Cut yarn into one-yard lengths, one for each child.

What to Do

1. Have the children color and cut out the garland figures from page 54 on the outer solid lines.
2. Help them fold and glue the figures over the yarn. Suggest that they space the items a few inches apart before gluing.
3. Maintain an exciting tone in the classroom as the children work on this project. Repeat the memory verse several times. Play tapes with praise music or lead the children in singing or humming favorite praise choruses.
4. Either create a display in your classroom with the garlands or allow the children to take home their garlands for Easter decorations.
5. Close with prayer.

Prayer

Jesus rose from the grave, and I am glad. I praise You, God! Amen.

Bible Lesson

Easter
Mark 15:21–16:20

Prayers of Praise

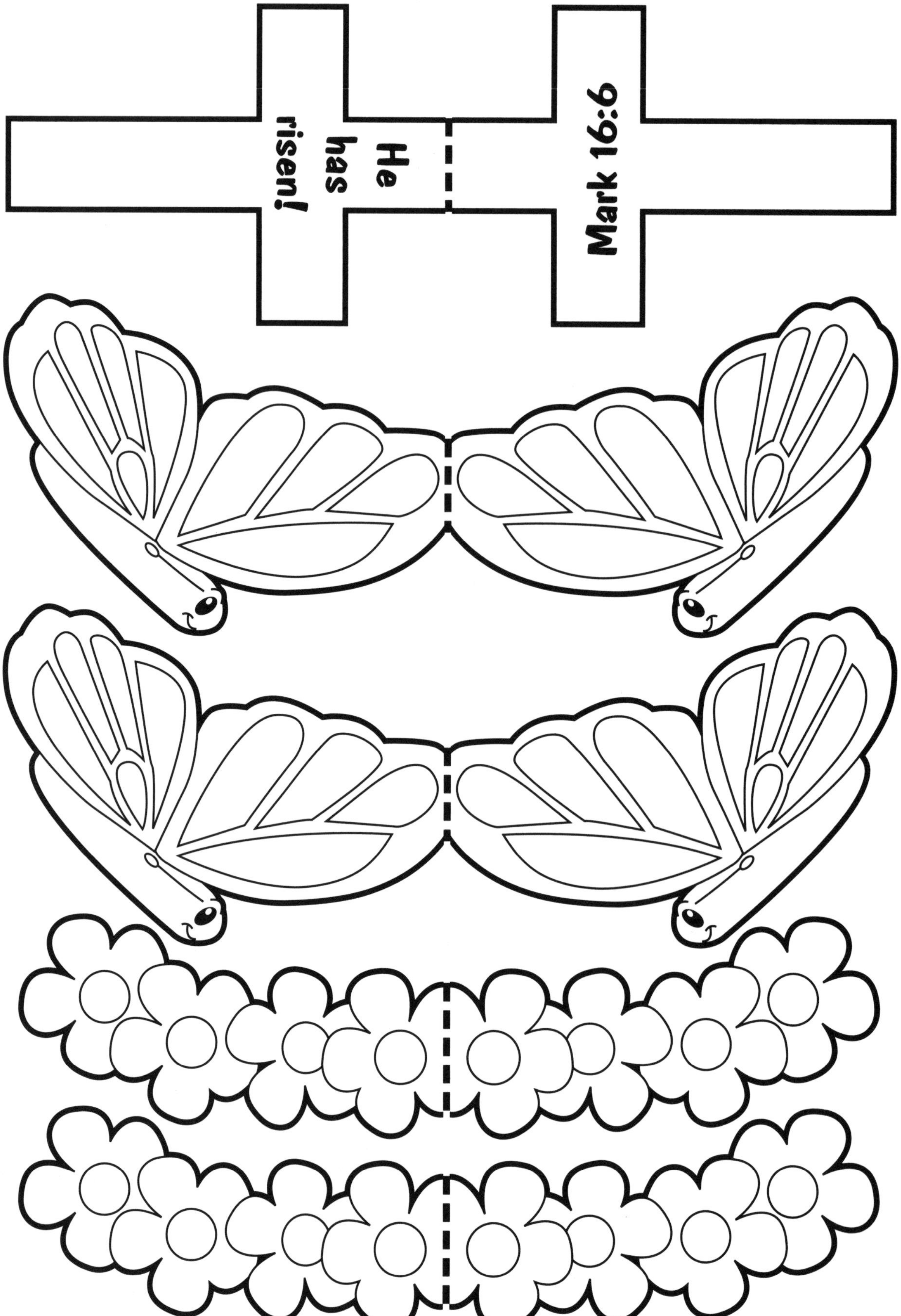
He has risen!
Mark 16:6

HAPPY FROG

Prayer Thought

I am happy because of God.

Memory Verse

Rejoice and be glad.

~ Matthew 5:12

What You Need

- page 56, duplicated
- crayons
- scissors

Before Class

Duplicate the frog pattern on card stock for each child. You may want to cut out the frogs for younger children.

What to Do

1. Have the children color and cut out the frogs. As they work, read the prayer poem to them. Ask, **Do you know why the frog is so happy? Because he's jumping and playing, his favorite thing to do. What do you do that makes you happy?**
2. Help the children fold the frogs' legs on the fold lines.
3. Show how to press down on the back edge of the frogs and let them go to make them jump.
4. Say, **Our happy frogs will remind us to be happy, rejoice and be glad. Let's praise God for the happiness in our lives.** Close with prayer.

Prayer

God, You make me so happy. I will rejoice and be glad every day. Amen.

Bible Lesson

Jesus tells how to be happy.
Matthew 5:1-2

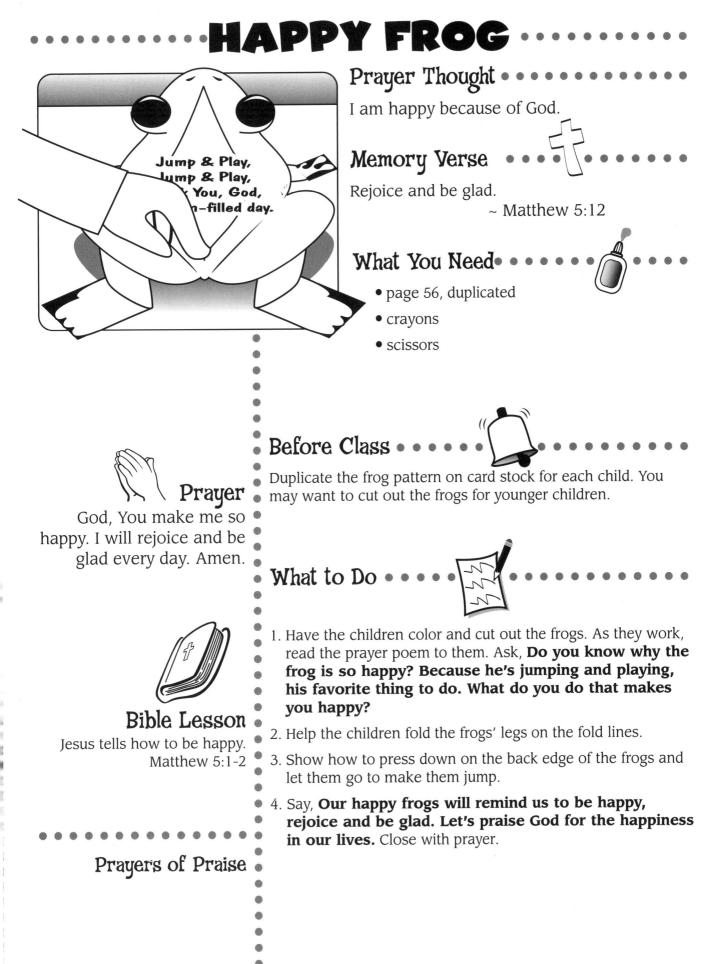

Prayers of Praise

Jump & Play,
Jump & Play,
Thank You, God,
For a fun-filled day.

MAGNIFYING GLASS GAME

Prayer Thought

My heart is filled with joy.

Memory Verse

My soul doth magnify the Lord.

~ Luke 1:46 KJV

What You Need

- page 58, duplicated
- magnifying glass
- small items (see below)

Before Class

Arrange small items (pennies, seeds, grass blades, etc.) on a tray for the children to view with the magnifying glass.

What to Do

1. Show a magnifying glass. Say, **This is a magnifying glass. It makes things look bigger than they are because it magnifies them. Let's look at the pictures on the page. See how big the pictures look? Now let's look at some other things around the room.** Let the children take turns looking through the glass at all the items on the tray.
2. Talk about the meaning of "magnify." Say, **Magnify means to make things bigger, just like the magnifying glass makes things bigger. Our memory verse says, "My soul doth magnify the Lord." This means that we are so filled with love for God, we make Him look big and wonderful to all those around us. Our happiness fills our lives and the lives of everyone we see.**
3. Say the verse again with the children, then close with prayer.

Prayer

God, I love You so much. My whole heart and body are filled with joy. Amen.

Bible Lesson

Mary visits Elizabeth.
Luke 1:39-47

Prayers of Praise

My soul doth magnify the Lord.

Luke 1:46 KJV

MY BUTTERFLY

Prayer Thought

I am glad that I know God.

Memory Verse

Praise the Lord, for the Lord is good.

~ Psalm 135:3

What You Need

- page 60, duplicated
- yarn
- crayons
- bright tissue paper
- glue
- scissors
- tape

Before Class

Cut yarn into one-yard lengths. Cut tissue paper into small pieces.

What to Do

1. Instruct the students to color and cut out their butterflies carefully on the outer solid lines.
2. Allow the children to select bright bits of tissue paper and glue the paper to their butterflies.
3. As the students work, create an attitude of praise in the room. Say the memory verse and encourage them to repeat it after you. Ask the class to share praises from their lives (you may want to suggest a few to get started).
4. Show how to tape one end of the yarn length to the butterfly's head, on the underside.
5. If time allows, let the students fly their butterflies in the room as they repeat the memory verse.
6. Close with prayer.

Prayer

I am glad that You are my Lord, and I praise You. Amen.

Bible Lesson

The Book of Law Is Read
2 Chronicles 34:29-32

Prayers of Praise

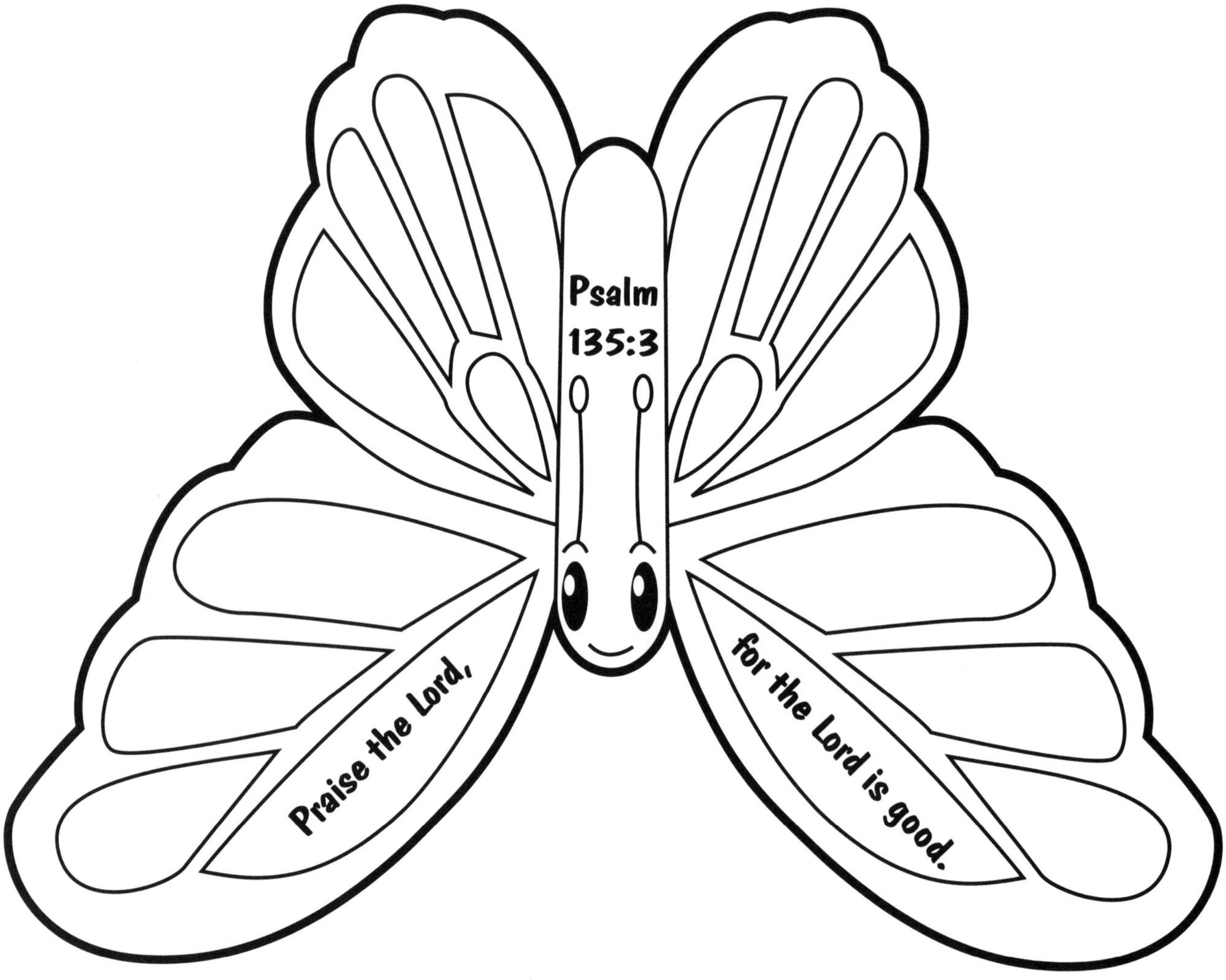
Psalm
135:3
Praise the Lord,
for the Lord is good.

NATURE BOOK

Prayer Thought

God's works are awesome.

Memory Verse

Come and see what God has done, how awesome his works.

~ Psalm 66:5

What You Need

- page 62, duplicated
- tape
- staplers
- crayons
- sealable plastic sandwich bags
- nature items (see below)

Before Class

Staple together five sandwich bags (on the left sides) for each student. Keep the open ends upward. Cover the staples with tape to avoid injury. Trace one book cover onto white paper for each student (use the outline only) and cut out to use as the back covers of the books. To fill the bags, you will need to provide nature items (leaves, rocks, bark, flowers, etc.) or pictures of nature items. Even better, plan a nature walk so the children can gather their own treasures.

What to Do

1. Have the children color the covers for their nature books. Build excitement over God's marvelous world by saying the memory verse and asking, **Who likes to look at leaves on the trees? Does anyone like to collect rocks or seashells? Let's make a special book so that we can collect some of the wonderful things God has made.**
2. After the children finish coloring, go around and help them staple the front and back covers together with the plastic bags between them. Show how to cover the staples with tape.
3. Either let the children choose some nature items you have brought, or go outside for a nature walk to collect items. Show how to put the nature items inside the plastic bags.
4. Afterward, ask each child to share a nature item and say, **This** (rock) **is one of God's awesome creations.**
5. Close with prayer.

Prayer

Dear God, I love to discover the awesome and wonderful things You put in Your world. Amen.

Bible Lesson

Creation
Genesis 1

Prayers of Praise

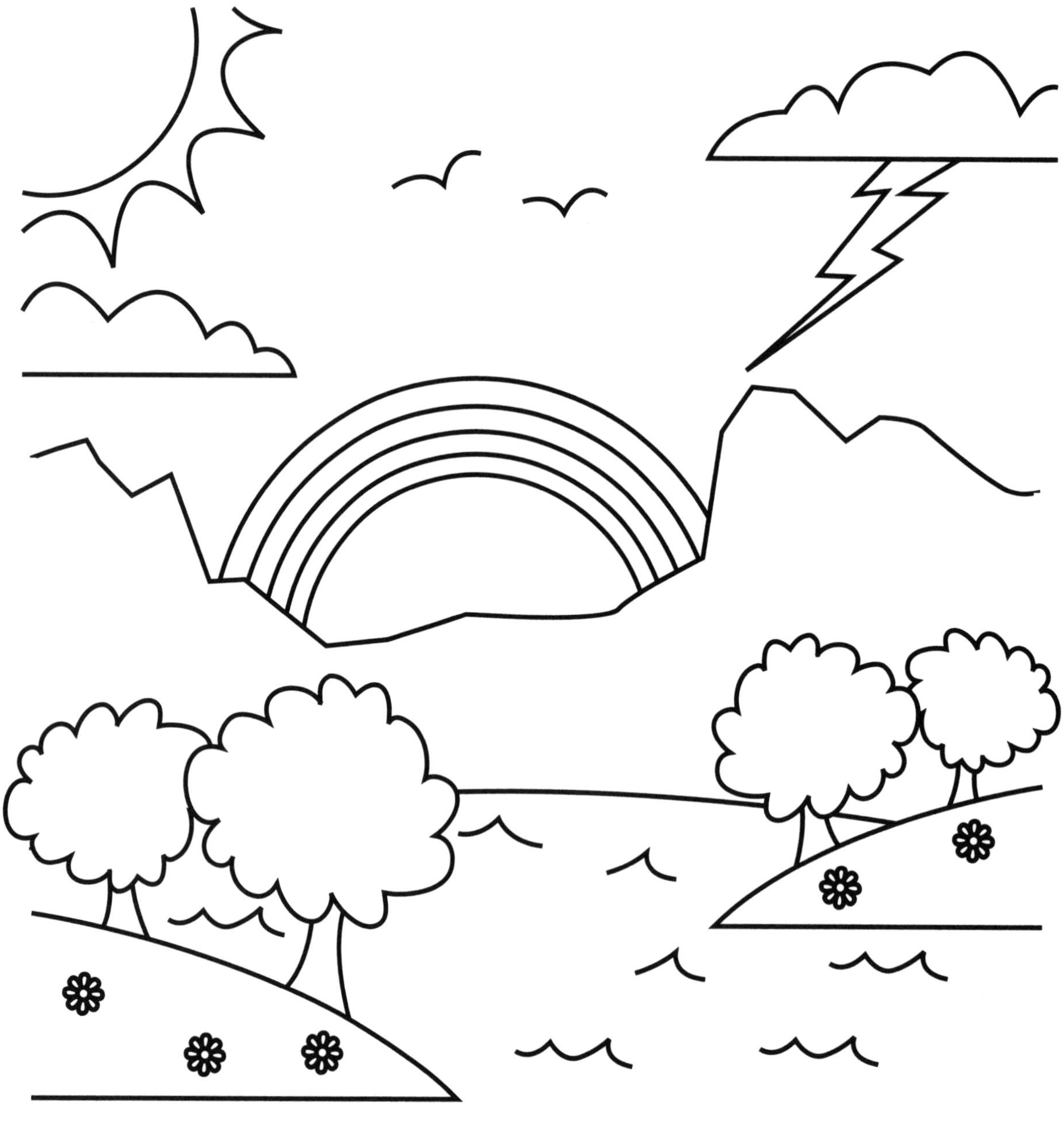

Come and see what God has done, how awesome his works. - Psalm 66:5

PERSISTENT PRAYER PUZZLE

Prayer Thought

God will answer my prayers according to His will.

Memory Verse

My heart rejoices in the Lord.

~ 1 Samuel 2:1

What You Need

- page 64, duplicated
- crayons
- glue
- construction paper
- scissors
- envelopes

Before Class

No preparation is required.

What to Do

1. As you tell the children about Hannah's fervent prayer, be sure to stress that God will answer our prayers according to His will. Build an atmosphere of praise as you tell students that Hannah received an answer to her prayer. Say, **Sometimes we think we know how and when God should answer our prayers. But we need to trust that He knows what is best for us. We should always praise God for answered prayer, whether it was the answer we thought we should receive or not.**
2. Have the students color the pages, then glue the pages to a sheet of construction paper for stability.
3. Allow the students to cut their puzzles apart on the lines. Provide an envelope for each child to carry the puzzle pieces home.
4. Take time to pray and thank God for answered prayer.

Prayer

God, I know You will answer my prayers in the way that is best for me. Amen.

Bible Lesson

The Birth of Samuel
1 Samuel 1

Prayers of Praise

My heart rejoices in the Lord.
– 1 Samuel 2:1

PRAISE PENDANT

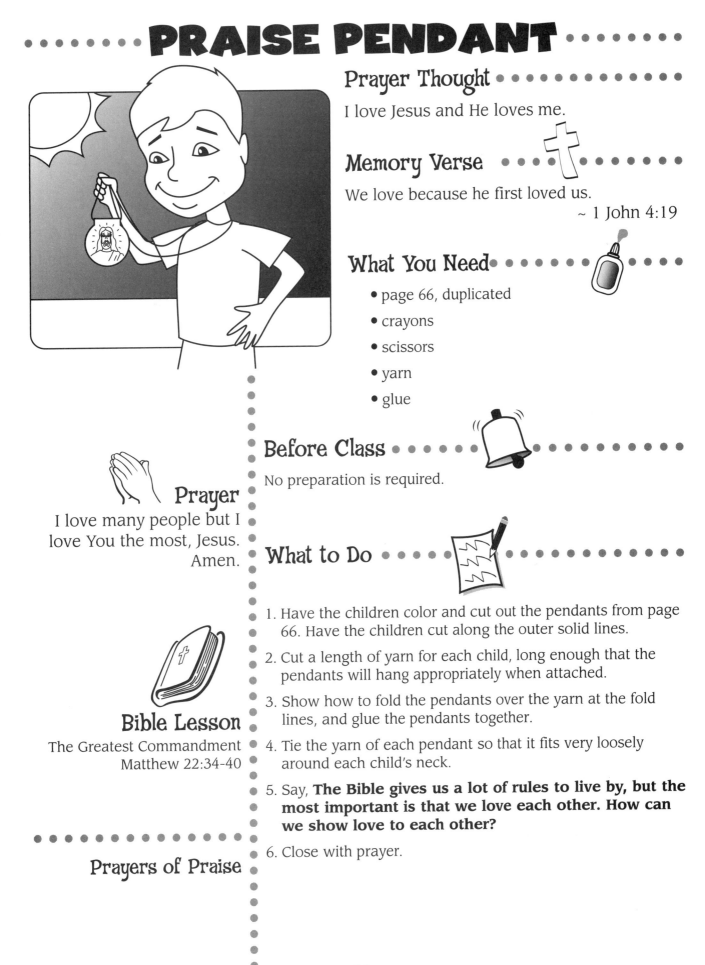

Prayer Thought

I love Jesus and He loves me.

Memory Verse

We love because he first loved us.

~ 1 John 4:19

What You Need

- page 66, duplicated
- crayons
- scissors
- yarn
- glue

Before Class

No preparation is required.

What to Do

1. Have the children color and cut out the pendants from page 66. Have the children cut along the outer solid lines.
2. Cut a length of yarn for each child, long enough that the pendants will hang appropriately when attached.
3. Show how to fold the pendants over the yarn at the fold lines, and glue the pendants together.
4. Tie the yarn of each pendant so that it fits very loosely around each child's neck.
5. Say, **The Bible gives us a lot of rules to live by, but the most important is that we love each other. How can we show love to each other?**
6. Close with prayer.

Prayer

I love many people but I love You the most, Jesus. Amen.

Bible Lesson

The Greatest Commandment
Matthew 22:34-40

Prayers of Praise

We love because
he first loved us.
1 John 4:19

PRAISE THE LORD WIND CHIMES

Prayer Thought

I can praise God through music.

Memory Verse

Blessed is he who comes in the name of the Lord.
~ Matthew 21:9

What You Need

- page 68, duplicated
- metal juice can lids
- construction paper
- crayons
- tape
- hole punch
- yarn

Before Class

No preparation is required.

What to Do

1. Talk about David and how he used music as praise. Say, **We can praise God in many ways, and music is a fun way to praise Him. How can we use music to praise God (congregational singing, choirs, piano, organ, etc.)? Let's make some wind chimes so we can praise God with music.**
2. As each child colors the illustration on page 68, repeat the memory verse.
3. Have the children glue the pictures to construction paper.
4. Show how to roll the pages into circles to form tubes and tape at the seams.
5. Help each student punch two holes across from one another at the top of his or her tube and attach the metal lids at the other end. At least three lids will be needed.
6. Show how to pull several yarn lengths evenly through the holes and tape the metal lids to the yarn.
7. Assist the children as they string the yarn through the holes at the top. Help them knot the yarn at both holes for hanging.
8. Close with prayer.

Prayer

God, I will do as David did and give You praise with music. Amen.

Bible Lesson

David, the Psalmist
The book of Psalms

Prayers of Praise

Blessed is he who comes in the name of the Lord.

Matthew 21:9

PRAYER BUDDY

Prayer Thought

I should always praise the Lord.

Memory Verse

Sing praise to him.

~ 1 Chronicles 16:9

What You Need

- page 70, duplicated
- chenille stems
- crayons
- glue
- scissors

Before Class

No preparation is required.

What to Do

1. Guide the children as they color the pieces to their Prayer Buddies and cut them out on the outer solid lines.
2. Show how to place the chenille stems on the back of one side of the body piece and glue at the arm and leg points.
3. Guide the students as they fold the bodies in half and glue them together with the chenille stems sticking out.
4. Show how to fold the hands and the feet over the ends of the chenille stems at the hands and feet, and glue to attach the stems.
5. Show the students how to bend the Prayer Buddy into prayer positions.
6. Repeat the memory verse and have the children use their Buddies to "help" them say the words.
7. Close with prayer.

Prayer

I will always praise You, God, even when life is difficult. Amen.

Bible Lesson

Job's Second Test
Job 2:1-10

Prayers of Praise

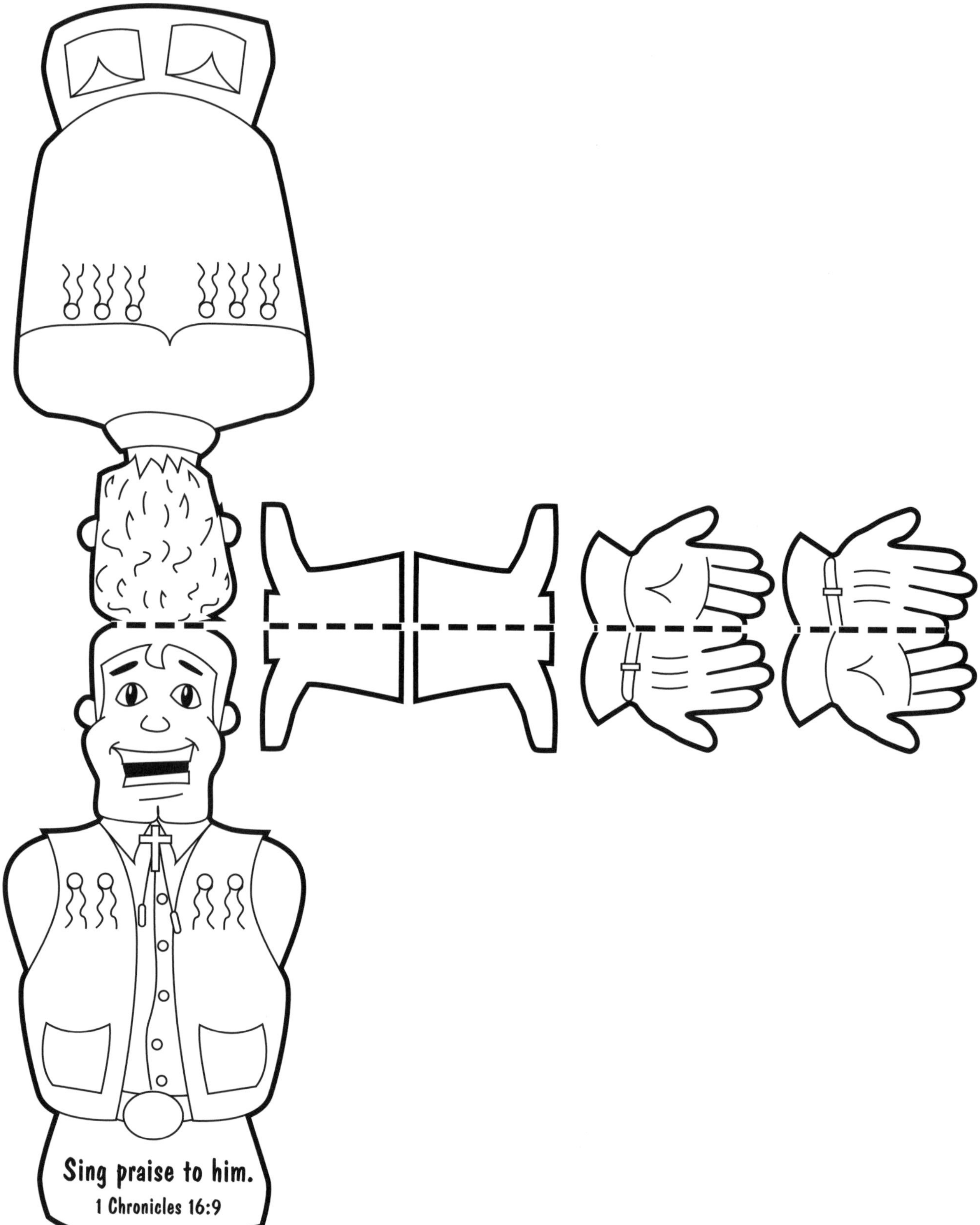

Sing praise to him.
1 Chronicles 16:9

STAINED GLASS WINDOW

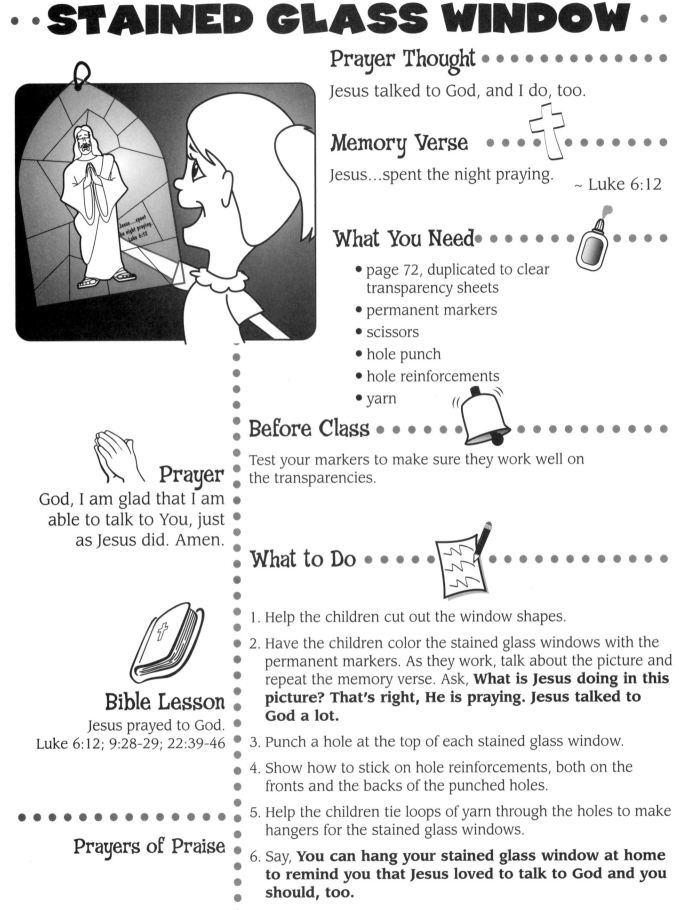

Prayer Thought

Jesus talked to God, and I do, too.

Memory Verse

Jesus...spent the night praying.
~ Luke 6:12

What You Need

- page 72, duplicated to clear transparency sheets
- permanent markers
- scissors
- hole punch
- hole reinforcements
- yarn

Before Class

Test your markers to make sure they work well on the transparencies.

What to Do

1. Help the children cut out the window shapes.
2. Have the children color the stained glass windows with the permanent markers. As they work, talk about the picture and repeat the memory verse. Ask, **What is Jesus doing in this picture? That's right, He is praying. Jesus talked to God a lot.**
3. Punch a hole at the top of each stained glass window.
4. Show how to stick on hole reinforcements, both on the fronts and the backs of the punched holes.
5. Help the children tie loops of yarn through the holes to make hangers for the stained glass windows.
6. Say, **You can hang your stained glass window at home to remind you that Jesus loved to talk to God and you should, too.**
7. Close with prayer.

Prayer

God, I am glad that I am able to talk to You, just as Jesus did. Amen.

Bible Lesson

Jesus prayed to God.
Luke 6:12; 9:28-29; 22:39-46

Prayers of Praise

Jesus...spent
the night praying.
Luke 6:12

STAR PRAISE

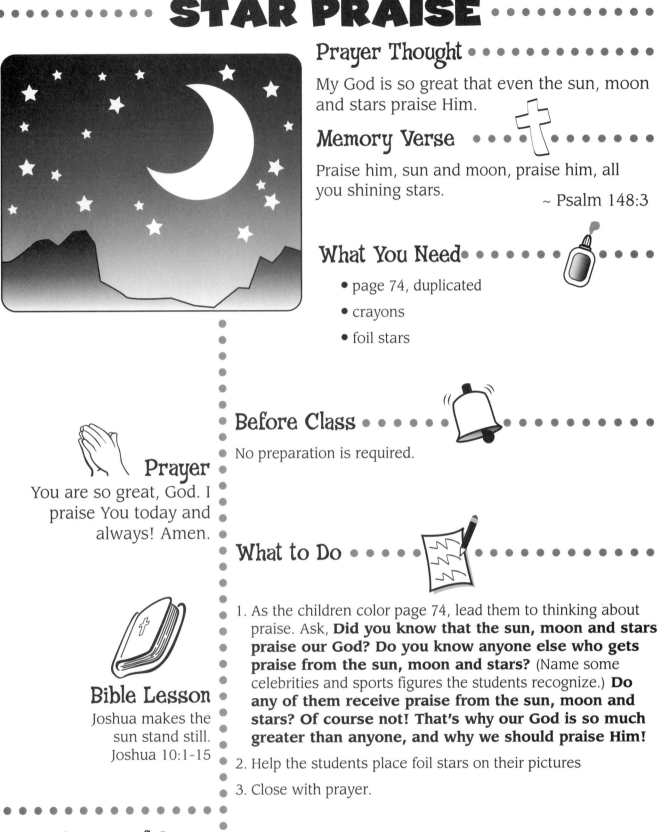

Prayer Thought

My God is so great that even the sun, moon and stars praise Him.

Memory Verse

Praise him, sun and moon, praise him, all you shining stars.

~ Psalm 148:3

What You Need

- page 74, duplicated
- crayons
- foil stars

Before Class

No preparation is required.

What to Do

1. As the children color page 74, lead them to thinking about praise. Ask, **Did you know that the sun, moon and stars praise our God? Do you know anyone else who gets praise from the sun, moon and stars?** (Name some celebrities and sports figures the students recognize.) **Do any of them receive praise from the sun, moon and stars? Of course not! That's why our God is so much greater than anyone, and why we should praise Him!**
2. Help the students place foil stars on their pictures
3. Close with prayer.

Prayer

You are so great, God. I praise You today and always! Amen.

Bible Lesson

Joshua makes the sun stand still.
Joshua 10:1-15

Prayers of Praise

Praise him, sun and moon, praise him, all you shining stars.

Psalm 148.3

CALL ON GOD

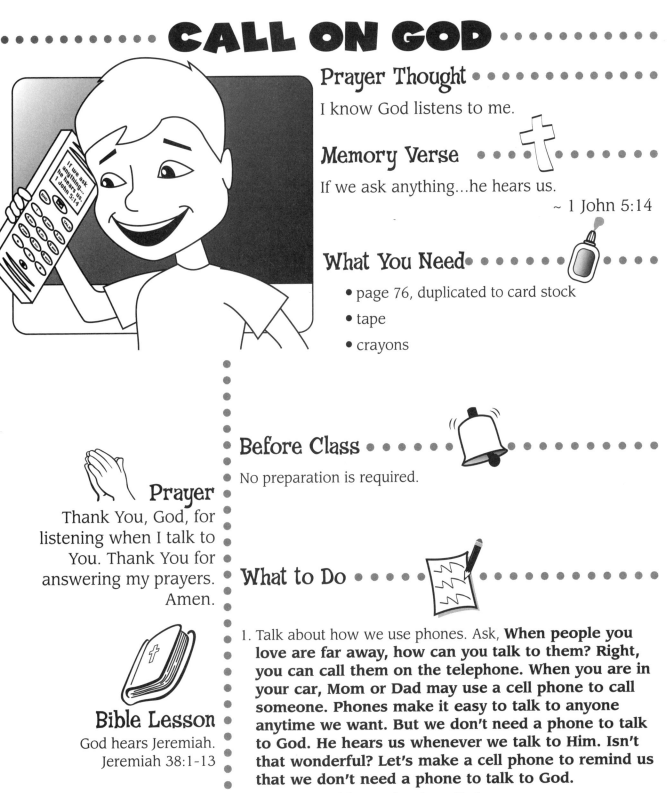

Prayer Thought

I know God listens to me.

Memory Verse

If we ask anything...he hears us.

~ 1 John 5:14

What You Need

- page 76, duplicated to card stock
- tape
- crayons

Prayer

Thank You, God, for listening when I talk to You. Thank You for answering my prayers. Amen.

Bible Lesson

God hears Jeremiah.
Jeremiah 38:1-13

Prayers of Thanks

Before Class

No preparation is required.

What to Do

1. Talk about how we use phones. Ask, **When people you love are far away, how can you talk to them? Right, you can call them on the telephone. When you are in your car, Mom or Dad may use a cell phone to call someone. Phones make it easy to talk to anyone anytime we want. But we don't need a phone to talk to God. He hears us whenever we talk to Him. Isn't that wonderful? Let's make a cell phone to remind us that we don't need a phone to talk to God.**
2. Have the children color the cell phones.
3. Help them fold the pages on the dashed lines and tape the seams.
4. Let the children pretend to call each other.
5. Then say, **Now, let's put down our phones and bow our heads. We can talk to God without using a telephone, anytime we want!**
6. Close with prayer.

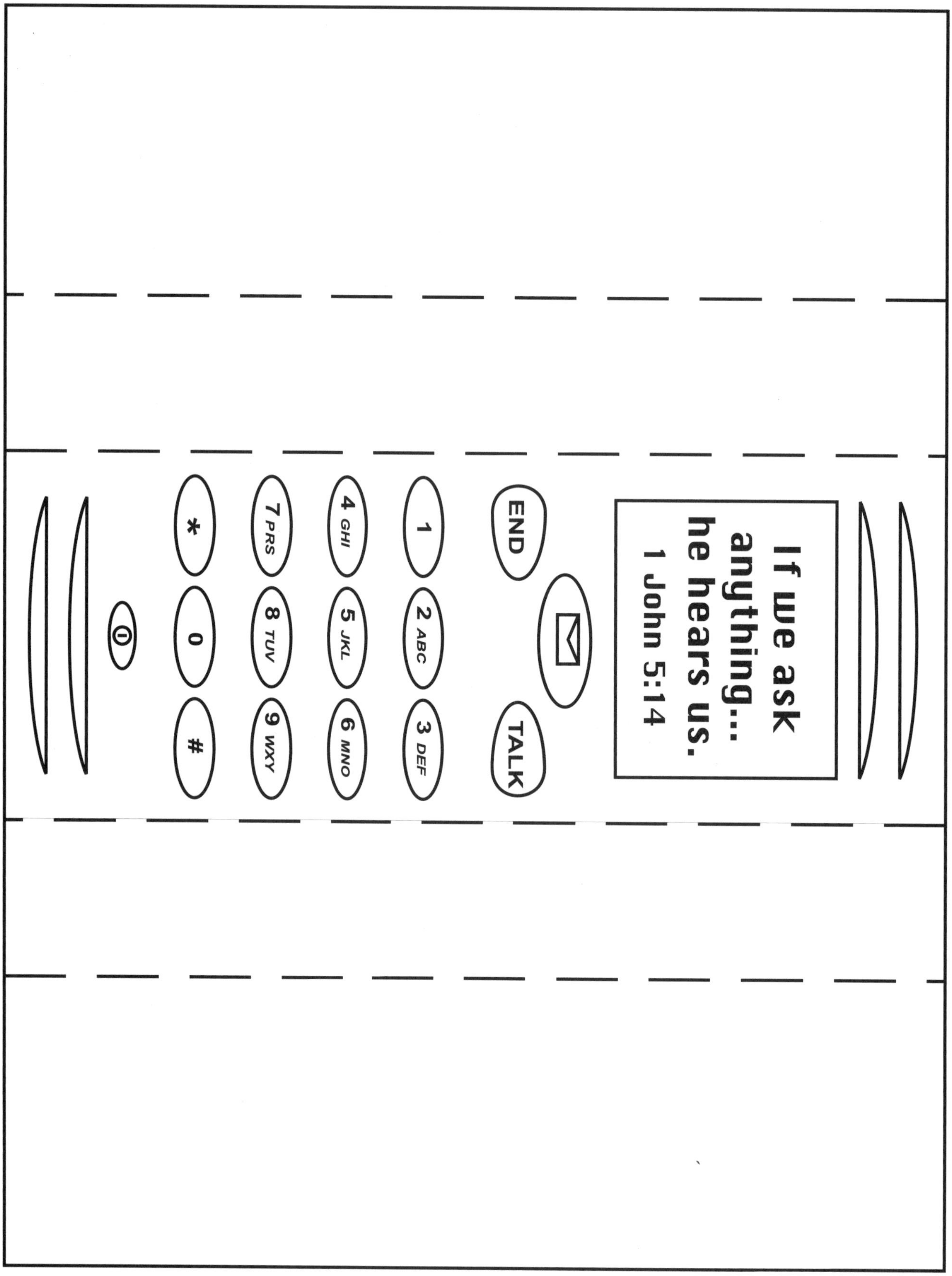
If we ask
anything...
he hears us.
1 John 5:14
END
TALK
1
2 ABC
3 DEF
4 GHI
5 JKL
6 MNO
7 PRS
8 TUV
9 WXY
*
0
#

FIVE TIMES TO PRAY

Prayer Thought

I will pray many times each day.

Memory Verse

Ask and it will be given to you.

~ Matthew 7:7

What You Need

- page 78, duplicated
- crayons

Prayer

I know You listen to me when I pray, God. I am so glad You are always there for me. Amen.

Bible Lesson

Ask, seek and knock.
Matthew 7:7-12

Prayers of Thanks

Before Class

No preparation is required.

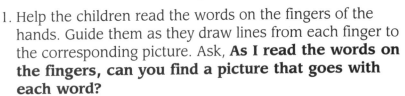

What to Do

1. Help the children read the words on the fingers of the hands. Guide them as they draw lines from each finger to the corresponding picture. Ask, **As I read the words on the fingers, can you find a picture that goes with each word?**
2. As the children color the pictures, discuss praying at various times of the day. Ask, **When are good times to pray?** Allow time for responses. Then say, **Any time is the right time to pray: morning, bedtime, mealtime, family time or playtime. Isn't it wonderful that we can talk to God any time we want?**
3. Repeat the prayer thought with the children, then close with prayer.

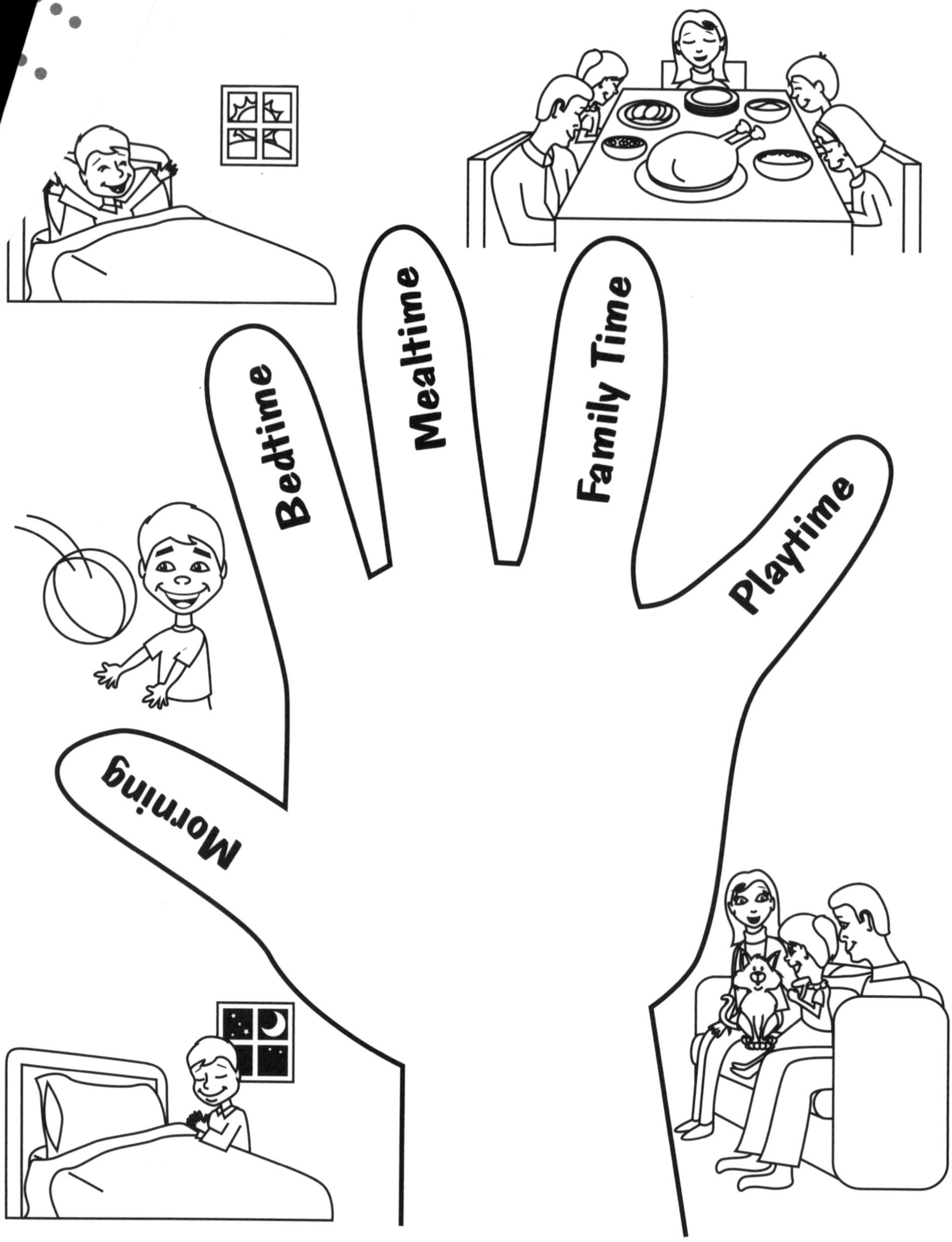

Ask and it will be given to you.

Matthew 7:7

HARVEST WREATH

Prayer Thought

I thank God for good food to eat.

Memory Verse

I give you every...plant and tree. They will be yours for food.

~ Genesis 1:29

What You Need

- page 80, duplicated
- paper plates
- scissors
- crayons
- glue
- yarn
- hole punch

Prayer

Thank You for good food to eat, God. You have given me everything that I need. Amen.

Bible Lesson

Daniel and friends eat healthy food.
Daniel 1

Prayers of Thanks

Before Class

No preparation is required.

What to Do

1. As the children color and cut out the items on page 80, have them tell you what the pictures of food are. Ask for more examples of good things God has given us to eat.
2. Help each child glue the pictures of food around the edges of a paper plate.
3. Show how to glue the memory verse in the center of the plate.
4. Allow the students to punch holes at the tops of the plates and add loops of yarn for hanging.
5. Close with prayer.

I give you every . . . plant and tree. They will be yours for food.
Genesis 1:29

IMAGE MIRROR

Prayer Thought

God made me special.

Memory Verse

God created [me] in his own image.
~ Genesis 1:27

What You Need

- page 82, duplicated
- poster board or construction paper
- crayons
- scissors
- glue
- aluminum foil
- yarn
- tape

Before Class

Cut out the center of the mirror on your copy only and use it as a pattern to cut out foil ovals for each child. If desired, you may glue the pages to poster board or construction paper before class time for stability. If using poster board, you may wish to cut out the mirrors because small hands may have difficulty with the stiff board.

What to Do

1. Help the children to cut out the mirror frame, if you didn't do it ahead of time.
2. Encourage them to say the memory verse as they color the frames. Say, **Do you know what the word "image" means? Look into a piece of foil and you will see your own image. That's how God made each of us: in His own image. Isn't that wonderful? God made us very special.**
3. Help the students glue the foil to the center of the mirror.
4. Give each child a piece of yarn and show how to loop and tape it to the top back of the mirror. Tell the students they may hang their mirrors at home to remind them that they were made in God's image
5. Close with prayer.

Prayer

Thank You for making me special and loving me. Amen.

Bible Lesson

God tells His people they are special.
Isaiah 43:1-7

Prayers of Thanks

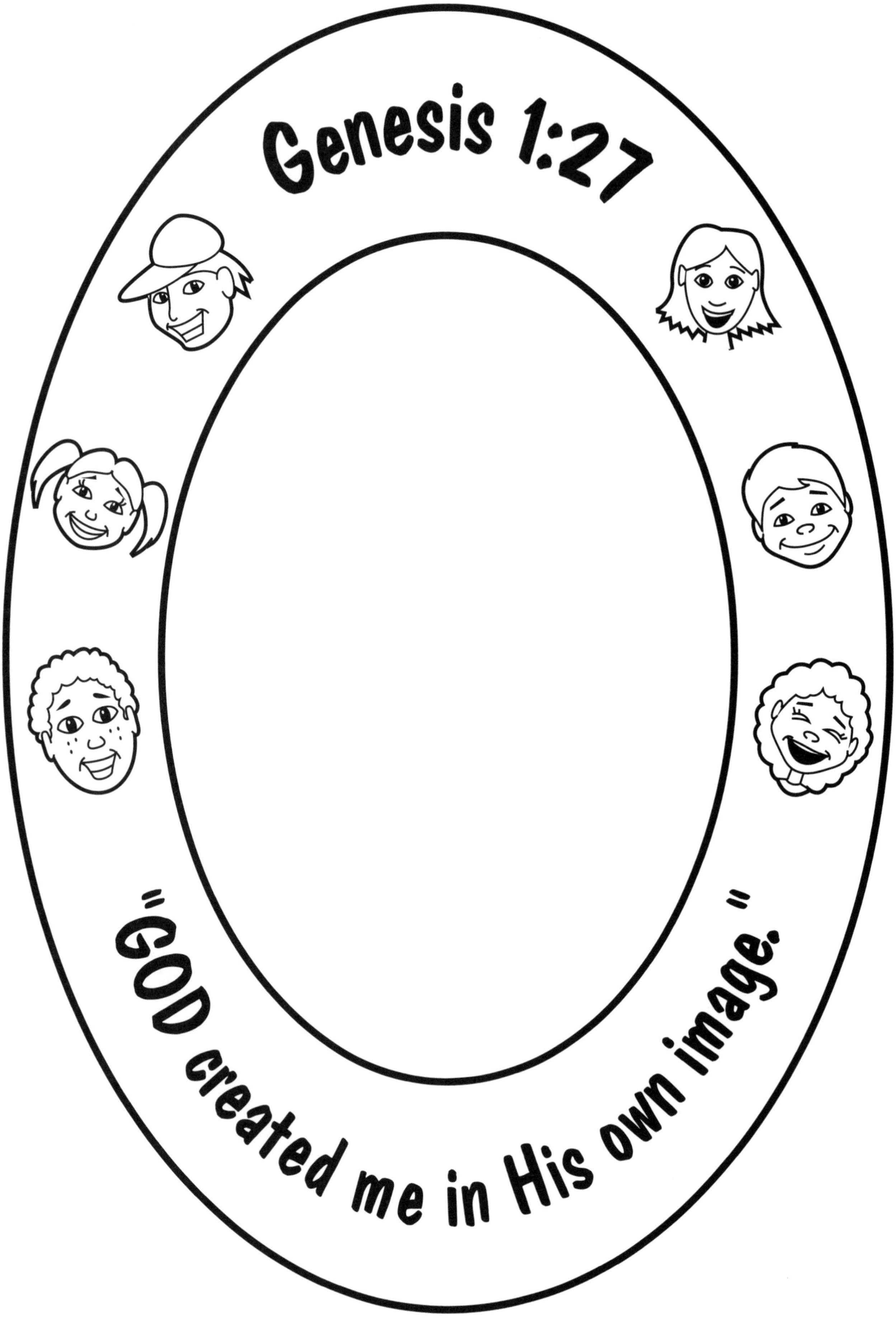
Genesis 1:27
"GOD created me in His own image."

JESUS FEEDS 5,000

Looking up to heaven, [Jesus] gave thanks.
Matthew 14:19

Prayer Thought

I can give thanks for my food.

Memory Verse

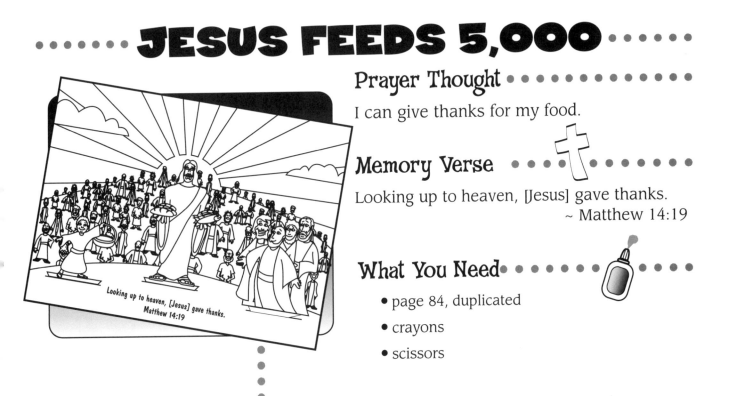

Looking up to heaven, [Jesus] gave thanks.
~ Matthew 14:19

What You Need

- page 84, duplicated
- crayons
- scissors

Prayer

Dear God, thank You for the food You give me to eat. Amen.

Bible Lesson

Jesus feeds 5,000.
Matthew 14:13-21

Prayers of Thanks

Before Class

Cut the slits in the hill scene. You might want to cut out the figures for younger children.

What to Do

1. Review the story of Jesus feeding the 5,000. Say, **The disciples didn't know how they were going to feed all the people. But Jesus and the little boy had faith that if they prayed to God, He would take care of everything. You can talk to God and ask Him to help you, too.**
2. Have the children color the hill scene and story figures, then cut out the figures.
3. Show how to retell the story by sliding the story figures into the slits in the scene. Say, **Let's put the figures in the scene and tell the story of Jesus praying to God so He could feed more than 5,000 people with just one lunch.**
4. Repeat the prayer thought with the children, then close with prayer.

Looking up to heaven, [Jesus] gave thanks.
Matthew 14:19

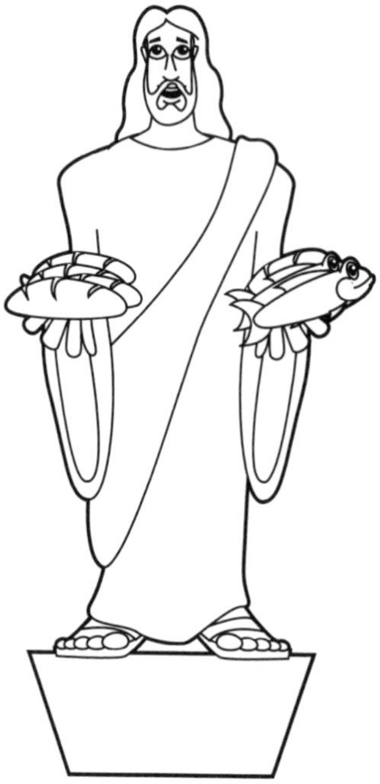

NEVER ALONE SWITCH COVERS

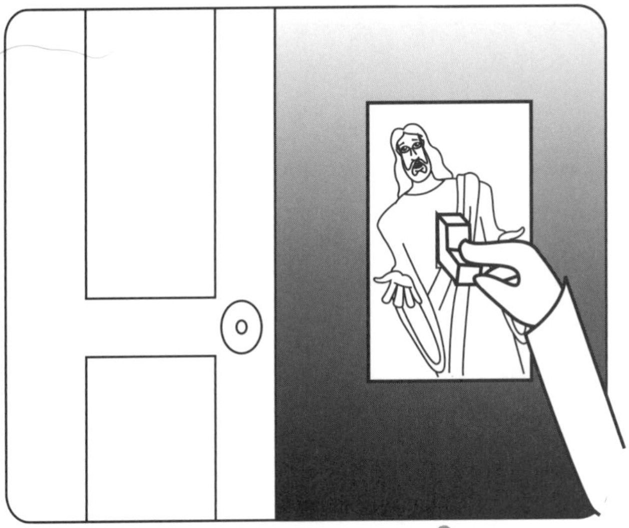

Prayer Thought

I am thankful that God is with me always.

Memory Verse

I am with you always.
~ Matthew 28:20

What You Need

- page 86, duplicated
- crayons
- scissors

Before Class

No preparation is required.

What to Do

1. Help the students cut out the two light switch covers from page 86 on the outer solid lines.
2. As they color the illustrations, help them learn the memory verse. Remind them that Jesus is with them, even at night when they are sleeping or when they are afraid in the dark. Say, **Tape one of these covers to the light switch in your bedroom and you will be reminded that Jesus is with you all of the time (suggest that they check with a parent before hanging the covers at home).**
3. Help the students cut out the center sections of the covers to make a place for the light switches to poke through.
4. Close with prayer.

Prayer

I will never be alone because I know You are always with me, God. Amen.

Bible Lesson

Peter in Prison
Acts 12:1-19

Prayers of Thanks

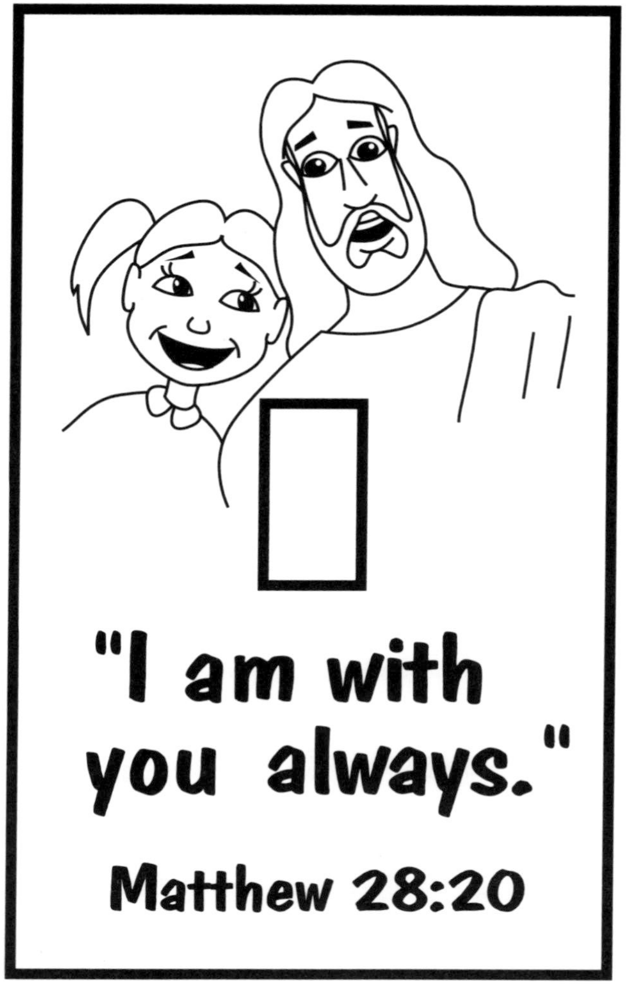
"I am with you always."
Matthew 28:20

PRAYER PLACE CARDS

Prayer Thought

God hears my prayers and answers them.

Memory Verse

If you believe, you will receive whatever you ask for in prayer.

~ Matthew 21:22

What You Need

- page 88, duplicated
- crayons
- scissors

Before Class

No preparation is required.

What to Do

1. Help the children cut apart the place cards on the solid lines and fold them on the dashed lines.
2. As the children color, discuss the individual pictures. Ask, **What are the people doing in the pictures? Our Bible says that if we believe, God will answer our prayers. Where do you like to pray? How has God answered your prayers?**
3. After the children finish, say, **Take home your place cards and put them on your table to remind your whole family that God will answer your prayers.**
4. Repeat the prayer thought with the children, then close with prayer.

Prayer

Dear God, thank You for telling us in Your Word that we may ask You for whatever we want. You will always provide what we need. Amen.

Bible Lesson

Jesus and the Fig Tree
Matthew 21:18-22

Prayers of Thanks

God hears my prayers.
God hears
my prayers.
God hears
my prayers.
God hears my prayers.
God hears
my prayers.
God hears
my prayers.
God hears my prayers.
God hears my prayers.

SUMMER FUN VISOR

Prayer Thought

I am thankful for the seasons.

Memory Verse

Let there be lights in the...sky to separate the day from the night and...to mark seasons.

~ Genesis 1:14

What You Need

- page 90, duplicated
- scissors
- crayons
- tape
- yarn
- construction paper

Before Class

No preparation is required.

What to Do

1. Help each student glue page 90 to a sheet of construction paper.
2. As the glue dries, have them color the pictures on the visors. Praise God for the seasons as they work. Ask, **Isn't summertime fun? What is your favorite thing to do in the summer?**
3. Instruct the class to cut out the visors and the verse squares.
4. Show how to glue the verse squares to the underside of the visors.
5. Cut two lengths of yarn for each child and show how to tape each one to an end of the visor.
6. Tie a visor onto each student's head.
7. Close with prayer, thanking God for summer fun.

Prayer

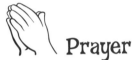

Thank You for all of the fun I have in the summer, God. Amen.

Bible Lesson

Daniel praises God for the seasons.
Daniel 2:19-23

Prayers of Thanks

Let there be lights in the...sky to separate the day from the night and...to mark seasons.

Genesis 1:14

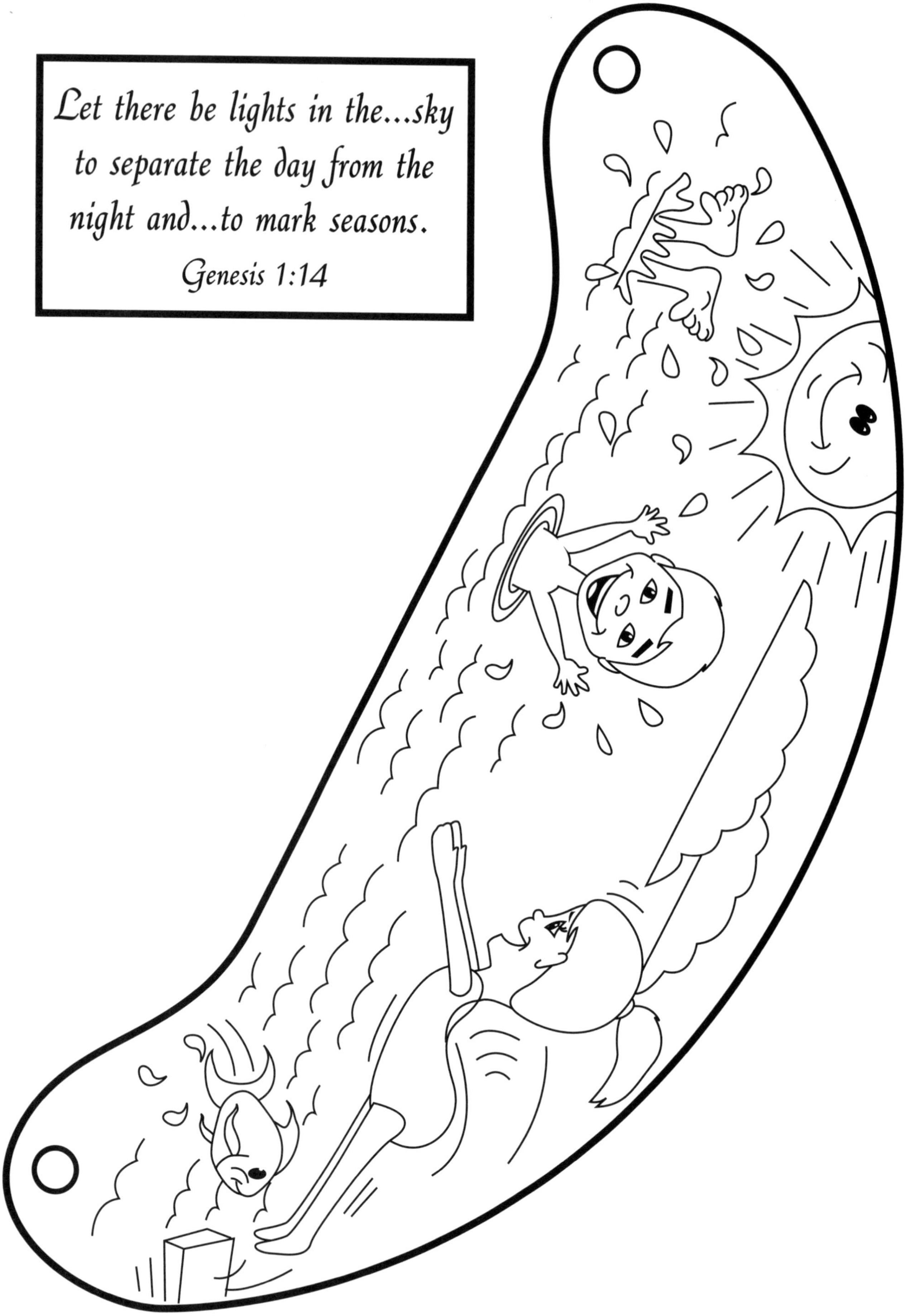

THANK-YOU CHAIN

Prayer Thought

I should say thanks to God for everything He gives me.

Memory Verse

I thank God.

~ 2 Timothy 1:3

What You Need

- page 92, duplicated
- scissors
- tape
- crayons

Prayer

Thank You for everything You give me, God, especially Your love. Amen.

Bible Lesson

Jesus and the children
Mark 10:13-16

Prayers of Thanks

Before Class

No preparation is required.

What to Do

1. Instruct the children to cut apart the six strips from page 92 on the solid lines. They may color before or after cutting.
2. Guide them as they trace over the words with crayons.
3. Help them loop the strips together, taping each one at the edge to form a chain as in the illustration above.
4. If desired, you may cut more strips from plain paper and have the students draw some more things for which they are thankful.
5. Either collect all of the chains and use them to decorate the classroom or allow the students to take home the chains to decorate their bedrooms.
6. Close with prayer.

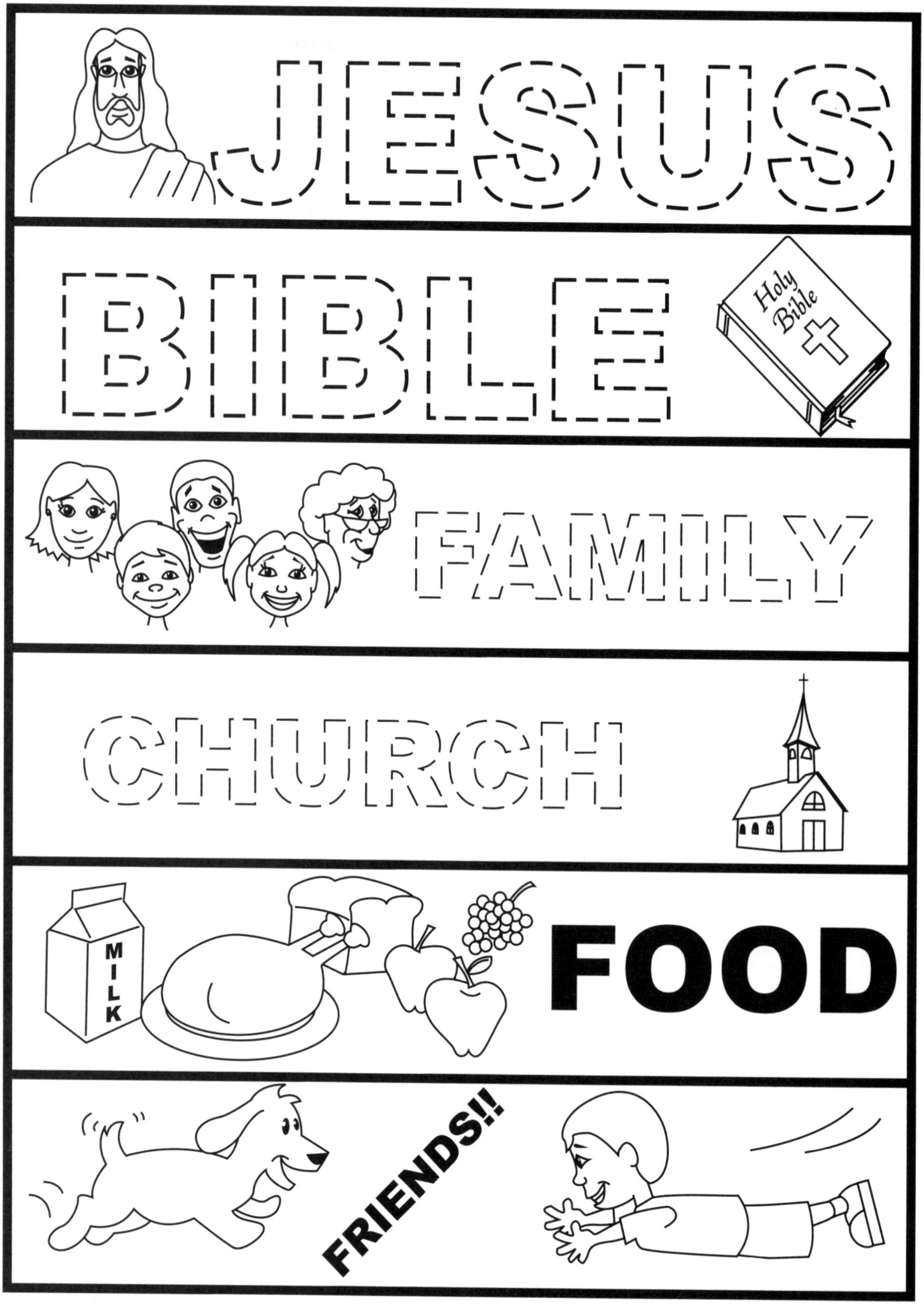
JESUS
BIBLE
Holy Bible
FAMILY
CHURCH
MILK
FOOD
FRIENDS!!

THANKFUL KITE

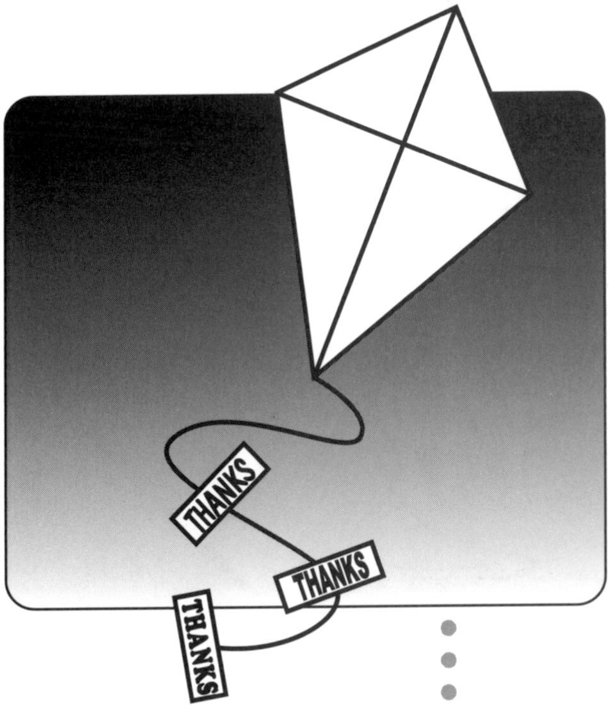

Prayer Thought

I am thankful for all that God does for me.

Memory Verse

Give thanks to the Lord, for he is good.
~ Psalm 136:1

What You Need

- page 94, duplicated
- crayons
- scissors
- yarn
- tape

Before Class

No preparation is required.

What to Do

1. Guide the children as they cut out the kites and the three tail pieces.
2. Have them color the kites. Then have them trace the letters on each tail piece.
3. Read the memory verse as the children work.
4. Help them tape the tail pieces to lengths of yarn and tape the resulting tails to the bottom edges of the kites.
5. Tape a length of yarn to the top edge of each kite so the students can "fly" their kites or hang them in their rooms. Tell the students that the kites will remind them to thank God every day.
6. Close with prayer.

Prayer

God, help me to always remember to thank You for all You do. Amen.

Bible Lesson

Jesus Heals the Lepers
Luke 17:11-19

Prayers of Thanks

Give thanks to the Lord
for he is good.
His love endures
forever.
Psalm
136:1

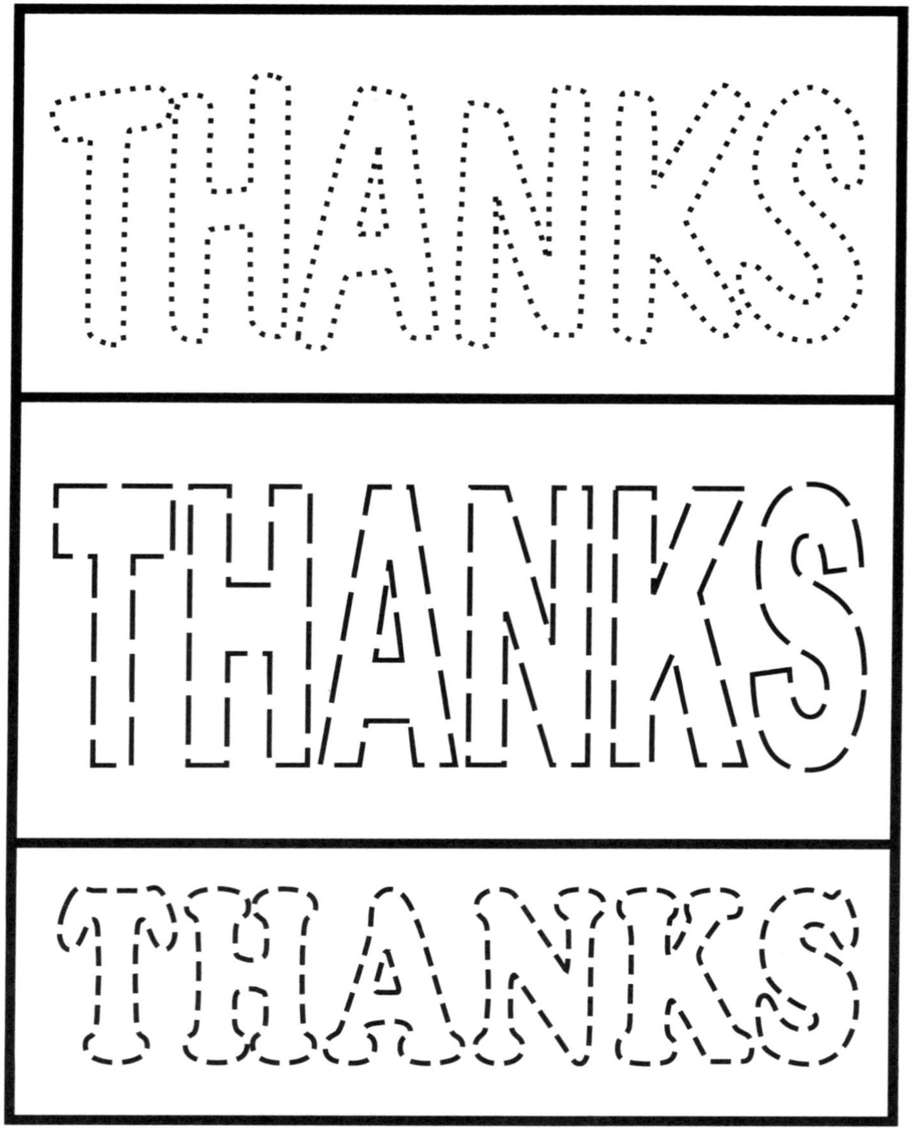
THANKS
THANKS
THANKS

THANKSGIVING PRAYER BOOK

Prayer Thought

I am thankful for many things.

Memory Verse

Give thanks in all circumstances.
~ 1 Thessalonians 5:18

What You Need

- page 96, duplicated
- crayons

Prayer

Dear God, thank You for my family, my church and my friends. Amen.

Bible Lesson

Timothy's mother and grandmother teach him about God.
2 Timothy 1:3-7

Prayers of Thanks

Before Class

No preparation is required.

What to Do

1. Help each child fold page 96 into quarters to form a book (fold the top down with the copy on the outside, then fold it together so "Thanksgiving Prayer Book" is on the front cover).
2. Help them read the words, then encourage them to draw pictures for each one. You may want to have an example on hand so slower workers can refer to your pictures to understand what to draw.
3. As they work, encourage the students to name other things for which they are thankful. Sing or hum tunes of thanks as they work.
4. Assist each child in writing his or her name on the front cover of his or her book.
5. Close with prayer.

JESUS

CHURCH

FRIENDS

FAMILY

Give thanks in all circumstances.

1 Thessalonians 5:18

Thanksgiving Prayer Book

This book belongs to

_ _ _ _ _